Asia Watches Japan
〈Revised Edition〉

Hideo Takemura

Toshiaki Matsumoto

Katsuhiko Odai

NAN'UN-DO

Asia Watches Japan ⟨Revised Edition⟩

Copyright © 2015

by
Hideo Takemura
Toshiaki Matsumoto
Katsuhiko Odai

All Rights Reserved
No part of this book may be reproduced in any form without written permission from the authors and Nan'un-do Co., Ltd.

Preface

　このテキストの旧版 "Asia Watches Japan"（「アジアから見た日本」）は 2000 年 1 月 20 日に出版されました。皆さまよりご好評を頂き深く感謝しております。その後世界は予想もしなかった速度でグローバル化し、激変しました。リアルタイムで舞い込む世界の情報。はるか海を越えて交わされるビジネス・トーク。世界の共通語に一番近い英語が「日常語」となり、もはや「英語難民」なんて言っていられる時代ではありません。英語力と正確なグローバル的な視野を持つ「真国際人」の登場が強く望まれています。今回の新版（本書）の主旨は、いかにしてアジアの情勢に敏感になれるのかを問うています。旧版から 14 年が経ち、今日の政界・経済界・社会情勢は、まるで「情報工場」のように瞬時に情報を吐き出しています。そうした時代の要請ともいうべきものに応えて編纂されたのが本書「アジアから見た日本＜改訂版＞」です。

　例えば、旧版には「日米防衛協力のための指針（ガイドライン）の新たな合意で、米軍が地域紛争に対処する際に、それを支援する日本部隊の役割が拡大することになっており、このような合意は平和憲法である日本国憲法に違反する恐れがある」と論評されています。さらに経済面では「日本と韓国が自由貿易圏を作ればどうなるのか」この種の話題を取り上げた記事が数本ありました。何はともあれ当時日本のＧＮＰはアジア全部のそれの合計を上回っていたのですから、日本の動向は大いに気になるところだったのでしょう。

　"Japan's economic growth showed no signs of slowing at the end of the 1980s ... turning the nation into a true superpower."（「日本の経済成長は、1980 年代の末期になっても衰えを見せる気配はなく…日本を真の超大国にした」）＜タイム誌、1988 年 7 月 4 日＞と日本は世界から "superpower" と称されるようになっていました。それから 26 年、日本は今まで経験したことのない索然とした「内憂外患」に悩まされています。この度、閣議決定された「集団的自衛権」(right of collective self-defense) について海外メディアはどう報じているのでしょうか。中国の「新華社通信」は「熱狂的で、近視眼的な政治家たちにより、日本が不必要な戦争に巻き込まれる危険がある」と音吐朗朗と語っています。韓国の「朝鮮日報」は「集団的自衛権行使の要件が曖昧である」と少々弛緩した論調で記述しています。では、アメリカはどう見ているのでしょうか。"ウォールストリート・ジャーナル" は「日本の安全保障の歴史的大転換を、憲法の改正でなく、解釈変更で行った安倍首相には批判が集まっている」と日本の野党の所見に近似した論調です。このテキストに収録されたアジア 16 ヶ国の最近の主要記事が、どのように日本を見ているのか、「歴史の中で事件を描き出し、危機を予見するという手法」には見事なものがあります。時代のターニングポイントを英語でダイレクトに読むことは、簡単な作業ではありません。何を読むか、どう読むかを学習しなければなりません。読んでいる中にアジアをモノにする攻略法がわかってきます。

　具体的にその手順を説明しますと…まず記事のアウト・ラインを把握するために、いわば記事の俯瞰図を知るために、Close-up に目を通してください。次に名セリフとも言える記事の核心を突いたPunch Line を読んで良質の英文を味わってください。次に Word Check 1、2 でボキャブラリー・テストをしてみましょう。Word Check 2 は、記事を読み終えた段階で取り組んでもかまいません。そこ

で、いよいよ本文です。中には難解な記事もあります。途中で諦めることなく、蟄伏することなく、アグレッシブに突き進んでください。英語をモノにするにはその道しかありません。"Give it a Try!" さて、次にはメディアの英文ライティング・スタイルを学ぶために、Structure & Writing Expression を読んでください。報道文特有の文体が理解できるようになっています。次に本文をどれだけ理解出来たかを知るために Comprehension に取り組んでください。そして最後に「解説」を読み、記事の背景に隠れているものを知ること…いわば「借景」のようなものですが、実は、これが「時事英語」を学ぶうえで、一番大切なことなのです。大いにこのコラムを利用してください。このテキストを作成した者の中に2人の元プロのジャーナリストがいますが、彼らは今の日本の在り方をどう考えているのでしょうか。今、言えることはグローバル化された情報過多の「職場」で、必要な情報を適時に検索できる能力を培い、生き抜いていくにはジャーナリストらしい発想が必要になってくるだろう、ということです。

　特殊な語・句やメディアの用語にはできる限り細心に注を施したつもりですが、記事が広範囲にわたっているために、編者の思い違いがあるかもしれません。ご叱正、ご教示を頂ければ幸甚です。なお本書編纂にあたり、記事の収録に関しまして各情報機関からご快諾を頂き、深く感謝いたします。また、南雲堂・編集部の加藤　敦さんには、骨の折れる編集の労をとって頂きました。本当にご苦労さまでした。

2014年8月　盛夏

編著者を代表して　竹村日出夫

Contents

Unit 1	Value Alliance Called for in New 'Cold War' Era （韓国）		6
Unit 2	China Considers Remembrance Day for Defeat of Japan and Nanking Massacre （香港）		11
Unit 3	Japanese Thank Taiwanese for Disaster Aid （台湾）		16
Unit 4	China Defiant on Territorial Claims, Demands Respect （フィリピン）		21
Unit 5	Japanese Cuisine 'Oishii'! （ブルネイ）		25
Unit 6	Anime Festival Brings Japan Closer to RI （インドネシア）		30
Unit 7	Japan Looks to Malaysia to Globalise （マレーシア）		35
Unit 8	Deepening Vietnam-Japan Strategic Partnership （ベトナム）		40
Unit 9	Asia's Deep Wounds of War Need German-style Healing (1) （タイ）		45
Unit 10	Asia's Deep Wounds of War Need German-style Healing (2) （タイ）		50
Unit 11	Japan on Backfoot in Global PR War with China after Abe Shrine Visit (1) （ミャンマー）		55
Unit 12	Japan on Backfoot in Global PR War with China after Abe Shrine Visit (2) （ミャンマー）		60
Unit 13	Japanese Ear Surgery 3-Day Camp Concludes （ブータン）		65
Unit 14	Japan's Clothing Retailer Uniqlo to Buy More from Bangladesh （バングラデシュ）		70
Unit 15	Speaking the Same Language （インド）		75
Unit 16	Buddhist Values Can Thwart Threats to World Peace （スリランカ）		80
Unit 17	Japan's PM Pushes India Ties amid Sino-Japanese Tensions （パキスタン）		85
Unit 18	Why Are the Japanese So Fascinated with Anne Frank? (1) （イスラエル）		90
Unit 19	Why Are the Japanese So Fascinated with Anne Frank? (2) （イスラエル）		95

Unit 1
Value Alliance Called for in New 'Cold War' Era

東亜日報（韓国） March 20, 2014

Close-up

ウクライナ南部クリミア自治共和国のロシアへの編入が決まった。オバマ米大統領は、クリミア半島を事実上掌握(しょうあく)する現代ロシアの「皇帝」と呼ばれているプーチン大統領と電話会見したが、その解決の糸口はなく、ロシアを除く G-8 のリーダーと会談を持ち、ロシアへの制裁を検討することになる。旧ソビエト連邦崩壊後の新たな国際状況（冷戦）の中で、日韓の態度も当然変わっていかねばならないだろう。

Punch Line

It is time for South Korea to cool-headedly read the situation and make a strategic choice in order to protect its national interest, amid seismic changes in the international order.

（国際秩序の大きな変動の中で、韓国は国益を守るためにこの状況を冷静に読み取り、戦略的選択を迫られている）

Word Check 1

(1)~(10) の語・句の意味として最も適当なものを選択肢 (a)~(j) の中から選びなさい。

(1) treaty　　　　　　　　(a) 領土
(2) territory　　　　　　　(b) 介入する
(3) violation　　　　　　　(c) 併合
(4) annexation　　　　　　(d) 戦略
(5) intervene　　　　　　　(e) 制裁
(6) head-on collision　　　(f) 外交の
(7) sanction　　　　　　　(g) 正面衝突
(8) initiative　　　　　　　(h) 条約
(9) friction　　　　　　　　(i) 摩擦
(10) diplomatic　　　　　　(j) 侵害

Russian President Vladimir Putin signed a treaty that absorbs Crimea into Russia on Tuesday. Russia's relations with the United States and the European Union are showing signs of returning to the Cold War era. Depending on how the situation develops, major countries around the world could be forced to make a choice between being pro-Russia or anti-Russia for the first time since the dismantlement of the former Soviet Union. It's time for South Korea to cool-headedly read the situation and make a strategic choice in order to protect its national interest, amid seismic changes in the international order.

The latest incident, in which one country took another country's territory for the first time in Europe since World War II, is a violation of international law. No other state but Russia recognizes the result of the Crimean referendum that took place amid Russian troops' deployment to the region. Nearly 97 percent of the voters supported the annexation. The cause for Russia's annexation of Crimea is nothing but an excuse under which Moscow attempts to intervene in the domestic affairs of all former Soviet states.

Under a slogan of building "a strong Russia," Putin has been relentlessly pursuing an expansionist line based on Russia's economic growth, fueled by brisk exports of gas and oil. Although the U.S. has avoided head-on collision by passively intervening in the situation, the latest incident will likely make it impossible for Washington and Moscow to redefine their relations. U.S. President Barack Obama plans to hold an emergency meeting with leaders of the G-8 powers, except Russia, on the sidelines of the Nuclear Security Summit to be held in the Hague, Netherlands next week. They are expected to discuss further sanctions in addition to freezing bank accounts of ranking Russian officials and entry bans. However, it would not be easy to find an effective solution unless they are resolved to risk war.

Seoul's Foreign Ministry said Wednesday that it would not recognize Russia's annexation of Crimea. It has to make a difficult decision whether to join the sanctions. Joining the sanctions could deal a serious blow to the Park Geun-hye administration's Eurasia initiative aimed at increasing exchanges with Russia. Also, there is no guarantee that North Korea or China would try to protect its national interest at the risk of violating international law.

Seoul has to make a careful judgment about the situation, and also

has to align itself with its allies, with which it shares values of liberal democracy, market economy and human rights. Despite the friction between South Korea and Japan over past history, it is true that the neighbors share common values regarding their present and future
5 relationship. Russia, albeit a democratic state in form, is actually under the rule of Putin, who is a modern-day czar. If Putin's expansionist ambition is left unchecked, it will likely undermine the basis for peace in both Central Asia and the Baltic region. While closely cooperating with Washington, Seoul needs to exchange dialogue channels with
10 Tokyo as well. As South Korea will become the chair state of the U.N. Security Council next month, it will have more room to make diplomatic efforts.

align oneself with ~
~と同盟を組む

czar
（ロシアの）皇帝

chair state　議長国

U.N. Security Council
国連安全保障理事会

Structure & Writing Expression

<見出しの be 動詞の省略>

過去分詞は受け身を表す。受身形 "be ＋過去分詞" の be 動詞は省略される。規則動詞や一部の不規則動詞の場合、過去形と過去分詞形が同形であるが、見出しでは過去形は用いられないので、ほとんどが受け身を表す過去分詞と考えて差しつかえない。

（例）

Up to 700 (Are) Feared Drowned in Indian Floods

（インドで洪水、700 人も死亡か）

という見出しは、**Up to 700 people were feared drowned in two separate flood disasters in India.** という lead paragraph（記事の文頭）から取られている。

本文では：

Value Alliance (Is) Called for in New 'Cold War' Era

Comprehension

本文の内容と同じものは T、異なるものには F と答えなさい。

1. (　　) South Korea decided to be pro-Russia for the first time.
2. (　　) Russia recently achieved substantial economic growth via exports of gas and oil.
3. (　　) Russia wants to expand its territory by interfering with all former Soviet states.
4. (　　) Eight major countries will discuss the problem soon.
5. (　　) The writer suggested that South Korea (should) align itself with Japan.

Word Check 2

下線部と同じ意味となるものを記号で選びなさい。

1. Depending on how the situation develops, major countries around the world could be <u>forced</u> to make a choice between being pro-Russia or anti-Russia ...

    (a) discouraged　　　(b) expected　　　(c) compelled

2. The cause for Russia's annexation of Crimea is <u>nothing but</u> an excuse under which Moscow attempts to intervene in the domestic affairs of all former Soviet states.

    (a) more than　　　(b) only　　　(c) never

3. However, it would not be easy to find an effective solution unless they are <u>resolved</u> to risk war.

    (a) determined　　　(b) encouraged　　　(c) hoped

4. Russia, <u>albeit</u> a democratic state in form, is actually under the rule of Putin, who is a modern-day czar.

    (a) because of　　　(b) despite being　　　(c) as well as

解説

　2014年3月、オランダのハーグで行われた日米韓首脳会談の記者会見の場で韓国のパク大統領が見せた態度は全世界のメディアの注目を浴びた。隣国である日韓両国の首脳が就任以来1年以上も首脳会談ができなかったが、オバマ米大統領の仲介で開催に至ったのである。この記者会見で、安倍首相が笑顔を見せながらパク大統領に韓国語で「お会いできてうれしいです」と話しかけた。それに対して、パク大統領は安倍首相と目を合わせることなしに硬い表情で下を向いた。

　このシーンは動画として一瞬にして世界中に流された。韓国メディアは安倍首相が下手な韓国語で話しかけた、と言い、日本のメディアでは失礼な態度だと非難する評論家のコメントを採用するなど、互いに不毛な中傷合戦がまた始まった。

　こうなってしまったのは「歴史問題」という落としどころのない事柄に拘泥しているからだと言えるだろう。その事で重要な国際問題解決が後回しにされている…との視点で書かれたこの記事は、ウクライナとロシアの問題を採り上げ、クリミアのロシア編入により、米欧とロシアの対立関係が激化し、冷戦構造が崩壊して以来最大の危機を迎えたと解説。そして、この冷戦構造にも似た新しい国際関係の局面に立ち向かうには、同じ民主主義という価値観を持つ同盟国として日本と韓国の協力が必要であると説いている。パク大統領の頑なな態度とは裏腹に、実質的な協力関係を築こうとする動きが韓国側に見えてきた事で、日本も同じ土俵で協力関係が築ける可能性が出てきた。実質を重んじるこの基本思潮が生まれ出た事を大切にし、日韓双方の努力で大きく育て挙げていく事が今後、喫緊の課題となってくるだろう。

Unit 2

China Considers Remembrance Day for Defeat of Japan and Nanking Massacre

South China Morning Post（香港）February 25, 2014

 ## Close-up

中国は第二次世界大戦の日本の敗北と南京大虐殺事件を公式に認め、国家の記念事業にしようと考慮している。

 ## Punch Line

> China accused Japanese officials of making inflammatory statements aimed at denying or glorifying Japan's militaristic past, and said Japan should explain its strategic intentions.

（中国外務省報道官は、日本が過去の軍国主義を否定もしくは賛美することを目的として、扇情的な陳述を行っていると日本当局を非難した。さらに、日本は戦略的意図を釈明すべきであるとも語った）

Word Check 1

(1)~(10) の語・句の意味として最も適当なものを選択肢 (a)~(j) の中から選びなさい。

(1)	designate	(a)	侵略
(2)	commemorate	(b)	緊張関係
(3)	aggression	(c)	掻き立てる
(4)	tension	(d)	外交官
(5)	foreign ministry	(e)	記念する
(6)	expansion	(f)	引き合いに出す
(7)	stir up	(g)	指定する
(8)	diplomat	(h)	拡張
(9)	invoke	(i)	外務省
(10)	criminal	(j)	犯罪者

China's central government may designate formal days of remembrance to commemorate Japan's defeat in the second world war, and the Nanking massacre, state media reported yesterday, amid disputes over territory and historical wrongs.

The National People's Congress (NPC) is mulling making September 3 "Victory Day of the Chinese People's War of Resistance Against Japanese Aggression", Xinhua said, citing the legislature. The official Japanese surrender was signed aboard the USS Missouri in Tokyo Bay on September 2, 1945, and was followed by three days of celebration in China.

Lawmakers are also considering designating December 13 as a "national memorial day to commemorate those killed by Japanese aggressors during the Nanking massacre in the 1930s", Xinhua reported.

In both cases, a "draft decision" would be debated during a bi-monthly session of the NPC Standing Committee from Tuesday until Thursday, Xinhua said. The national legislature will convene in Beijing for its annual plenum next week.

Meanwhile, Beijing yesterday called Japan a "troublemaker" damaging regional peace and stability, firing back at earlier criticism from Tokyo over a spike in tensions in northeast Asia.

Foreign ministry spokeswoman Hua Chunying was responding to comments by Japanese foreign minister Fumio Kishida, who said that China's military expansion in the region was a concern. However, Kishida stopped short of calling China a threat.

Hua said at regularly scheduled news conference that China's military posture was purely defensive, and Japan was stirring up trouble with its own moves to expand its armed forces and alter its pacifist constitution.

She accused Japanese officials of making inflammatory statements aimed at denying or glorifying the country's militaristic past, and said Japan should explain its strategic intentions.

"I think everybody will agree with me that Japan has already become a de facto troublemaker, harming regional peace and stability," Hua said.

Hua's comments were the latest salvo in a war of words between the countries that has seen their diplomats invoke the villain from the Harry Potter books, Lord Voldemort, in describing each other's motivations.

Never warm, bilateral ties sunk in 2012 after Japan purchased the disputed Diaoyu Islands in the East China Sea. They are claimed by Beijing and Taipei, but controlled by Tokyo, which calls them the Senkaku Islands.

5 Tensions worsened further in late December when Japanese Prime Minister Shinzo Abe visited Tokyo's Yasukuni Shrine, the one which commemorates 2.5 million Japanese war dead, including 14 Class A war criminals from the second world war.

China contends that 300,000 civilians and soldiers died in the "rape
10 of Nanking;" a spree of killing, sexual assault and destruction, over six weeks after the Japanese military entered the then capital on December 13, 1937. Although some foreign experts put the death toll much lower, no respected mainstream historians dispute the massacre.

Never warm,
= Having never been warm,

Diaoyu Islands
釣魚諸島（尖閣諸島の中国名）

rape　略奪

Structure & Writing Expression

< 短い単語の活用 >

メディアの記事の中には、一見して見慣れない短い単語がある。特に「見出し」に多用される。長い単語を使ってスペースを無駄にしないように配慮されているためだ。

(例)

agreement = accord   /   assistance = aid

prohibit = ban   /   reveal = bare

support = back   /   arrest = nab

consent = nod   /   investigate = probe

criticize = rap   /   exchange = swap

relations = ties   /   increase = rise

そして、本文では consider の代わりに、見出しではないが、mull が使われている。

The National People's Congress (NPC) is mulling making September 3 "Victory Day of the Chinese People's War …"

Comprehension

本文の内容と同じものは T、異なるものには F と答えなさい。

1. (　　) The Second World War officially concluded on September 2, 1945.
2. (　　) The plenum of Chinese national legislature is held once a year.
3. (　　) Kusida said aloud that China was a threat to Japan.
4. (　　) Bilateral ties did not worsen despite Abe's visit to Yasukuni Shrine.
5. (　　) Historians agreed that the death toll of the Nanking massacre was around 300,000.

Word Check 2

下線部と同じ意味となるものを記号で選びなさい。

1. The official Japanese <u>surrender</u> was signed aboard the USS Missouri in Tokyo Bay on September 2, 1945, and was followed by three days of celebration in China.
   (a) victory　　　　　(b) submission　　　　(c) treaty

2. ... that China's military expansion in the region was a concern, although Kishida <u>stopped short of</u> calling China a threat.
   (a) refrained from　　(b) persisted in　　　(c) put off

3. China accused Japanese officials of making inflammatory statements <u>aimed at</u> denying or glorifying the country's militaristic past, and ...
   (a) disappointed at　(b) named after　　　(c) intended for

4. Although some foreign experts put the death toll much lower, no respected mainstream historians <u>dispute</u> the massacre.
   (a) emphasize　　　　(b) reveal　　　　　　(c) deny

解説

　この記事は北京で開かれた中国の国会に相当する全国人民代表大会で、米戦艦ミズーリ号上で日本の降伏調印が行われた1945年9月3日を中国の対日戦勝記念日とする事が決定された事。それに加えて代議員達が12月13日を日本軍が1930年代の南京攻略戦で30万人を虐殺した日として国民の記念日にしようと考えているとの新華社（中国国営メディア）の報道として伝えたものだ。記事ではこの他、人民代表大会後の中国政府記者会見で発表された日本批判をそのままストレートに伝えている。

　しかし、注目すべきは南京虐殺問題を採り上げ、中国政府が南京で30万人が虐殺されたとしているが、中国以外の専門家は死者の統計がもっと少ないとしていると付け加えている事だ。

　このような記事の書き方は香港メディアの現状を表していると言える。香港の有力紙「名報」編集長が2013年暮れに突然解任され、翌2014年2月26日に暴漢に襲われて背中と足を切り付けられ重傷を負うという事件が起きた。その原因について、香港メディアによると、襲われた編集長の新聞で当局を非難する記事を掲載した事がきっかけだとし、暗に中央政府の陰惨な圧力の存在を示唆する報道が主となっている。これら一連の事件が原因となって、報道の自由を求める記者たちのSNSを使ったアピールが盛んになされ、それを支援する香港市民達が数万人規模のデモを行うなど、2014年初頭から報道の自由をめぐって香港は騒然とした雰囲気にあった。この記事も、中央政府機関の報道をそのまま引用しつつ、最後にチクリと刺す手法をとったものだとすれば、民主主義不在の政治文化しか持っていない政府の圧力と香港メディアが報道の在り方をめぐってしのぎを削る軋轢の一端が見えた記事というべきだろう。

Unit 3
Japanese Thank Taiwanese for Disaster Aid

The Taipei Times（台湾）March 10, 2014

Close-up

東日本大震災から3年目を記念して、日本の「謝謝台湾活動実行委員会」＜謝謝台湾＞の会員たちは、台北の新都市、淡水で記念行事をとり行った。この会の活動の背景には、台湾が義援金、おおよそ2億6千万ドルを日本に寄付したという慈善の心がある。これはどこの国からよりも多額の義捐金であった。実行委員会は被災地の人たちの心が少しでも和むようにといろいろな創意工夫をこらしている。

Punch Line

> Kosaka said he and four companions visited Fukushima's disaster-stricken areas in November last year, and discovered that while many victims outwardly show a positive attitude and perseverance, they are still suffering.

（小坂さんと仲間の4人は昨年の11月福島の被災地を訪れた、多くの被災者たちは、外面では前向きな態度と頑張りを見せているようだが、一方内面ではまだ心に傷を負っているようだ、と小坂さんは語った）

Word Check 1

(1)~(10) の語・句の意味として最も適当なものを選択肢 (a)~(j) の中から選びなさい。

(1) donation   (a) 絆でつなぐ
(2) reminder   (b) 再会する
(3) bond   (c) 置き去りにする
(4) envelope   (d) 寄付
(5) relative   (e) 親戚
(6) reunite   (f) 表面上は
(7) companion   (g) 忍耐
(8) outwardly   (h) 思い出させるもの
(9) perseverance   (i) 仲間
(10) leave behind   (j) 封筒

A group of Japanese organizers yesterday held an event in New Taipei City's Tamsui District (淡水) called "Thank you, Taiwan," to mark the third year since a major earthquake and tsunami struck Northeastern Japan, on March 11, 2011.

After the disaster, Taiwan donated about US$260 million in aid to Japan; the biggest donation made by any country.

Members of the "Thank you Taiwan" activities executive committee said the event served as a reminder that although three years have passed since the disaster, most of the stricken areas and victims have not yet recovered.

Participants at yesterday's event wrote blessings on colored paper, folded them into origami cranes and glued them to a paper board bearing the title: "Bonding hearts," which will be taken to the disaster-stricken areas to give victims moral support, said the committee's executive director, Kengo Kosaka, who is a freshman at National Taiwan Normal University's Institute of Management.

Rin Tatsukawa, a Japanese national and a senior at the university's Department of Chinese Literature, said that after the earthquake struck, she and her classmates had raised relief funds by collecting campus donations.

"One person gave two envelopes — each with NT$10,000 inside. I was so touched to see how the Taiwanese were helping my country," she said.

Manami Ono, from disaster-stricken Miyagi Prefecture, said she lived only 3 miles away from the ocean, and when the tsunami hit the area, she saw her senior-high and junior-high school campuses, as well as her friends and relatives' houses, wash away.

She said she was lucky that her house was not damaged, and that she was able to reunite with her family.

The reason she applied to National Chengchi University's Department of Journalism was because she wanted to visit Taiwan, the country which had helped Japan so much.

Kosaka said he and four companions visited the disaster-stricken areas in November last year, and discovered that while many victims outwardly show a positive attitude and perseverance, they are still suffering.

After three years, and with limited Japanese government aid, society has forgotten about those left behind, he said, adding that so many places still need long-term reconstruction.

However, the victims will not forget how the Taiwanese lent them a hand in a time of great need.

Structure & Writing Expression

\<hyphenated words\>

なるべくスペースを節約し、簡素な文章で表現するメディアの文体では、2語以上の語をハイフンで結び1つの品詞の働きをさせることがしばしばある。これは名詞の形容詞的用法（名詞＋名詞の形で、最初の名詞が形容詞の働きをする）とともにメディア英語の大きな特徴の1つである。

（例）

名詞＋過去分詞・・・state-owned business（国営企業）\<business owned by state\>

本文では：

＊ ... which will be taken to the disaster-stricken areas to give ...

＊ ... from disaster-stricken Miyagi Prefecture, ...

＊ ... he and four companions visited the disaster-stricken areas ...

Comprehension

本文の内容と同じものはT、異なるものにはFと答えなさい。

1. (　) No other country donates more money than Taiwan.
2. (　) Origami cranes will be sent to disaster-stricken areas.
3. (　) Rin Tatsukawa received much money by mail.
4. (　) Masami Ono appreciated Taiwan's aid to Japan, and decided to study in Taiwan because of it.
5. (　) Disaster survivors have thrived due to strong support by the Japanese government.

Word Check 2

下線部と同じ意味となるものを記号で選びなさい。

1. "... Taiwan," to <u>mark</u> the third year since a major earthquake and tsunami struck northeastern Japan on March 11, 2011.
   (a) measure   (b) spend   (c) commemorate

2. Members of the "Thank you Taiwan" activities executive committee said the event <u>served</u> as a reminder that although ...
   (a) functioned   (b) was held   (c) was called

3. Rin Tatsukawa, a Japanese national and a <u>senior</u> at the university's Department of Chinese Literature, said that ...
   (a) second-year student   (b) third-year student   (c) fourth-year student

4. "I was so <u>touched</u> to see how the Taiwanese were helping my country," she said.
   (a) astonished   (b) moved   (c) depressed

解 説

　インターネットの動画投稿サイトにアクセスすれば、今でも無数の東日本大震災に対する応援メッセージや、寄付を募るイベントなど、日本を支援しようとする当時の動画を見ることができる。世界各国の若者が中心となって、貧しい国、豊かな国を問わずに震災復興への援助金が集められ、みんな惜しげもなく金品を差し出してくれる様子は3年たった現在でも我々の胸を熱くする。

　中でも台湾は日本で芸能活動をしていた歌手や俳優、タレントなどが中心となって昼夜を問わずキャンペーンを繰り返し、「日本加油（日本がんばれ）！」という言葉とともにアメリカドルで2億6,000万ドル、日本円にして実に300億円もの義援金を贈ってくれたのである。それは世界中から集まった義援金の中でも群を抜いて多額であった。

　しかしながら、時の民主党政府は東日本大震災1周年記念集会には中国政府に気遣いをしたのか、台湾代表を正式に招待せず、犠牲者を悼む献花も他の一般の参加者と同等に扱ったのである。日本は日中国交正常化の条件として、台湾を正式な国家とは認めない立場をとっている。その意味では当時の政府の台湾に対する処置は論理的には間違っていなかったと言えるだろう。

　この記事は台湾に留学している、日本政府とは関係ない一般の日本人学生があくまで自主的に台湾の人達に感謝の意を表した事を採り上げ、それを温かい眼差しで伝えている。この記事に触れる事で改めて台湾の人達の心の広さと、わけ隔てない人間としての愛情を感じざるを得ない。

Unit 4
China Defiant on Territorial Claims, Demands Respect

The Manila Bulletin (フィリピン) March 9, 2014

Close-up

中国は、アジア太平洋地域の高まる緊張関係の中で、隣国との領土問題にかかわる紛糾には、一切妥協しない姿勢をとっている。中国の統治権は、アメリカとの関係が良好な基盤でなければならないと判断している。特に歴史と領土という本質にかかわる問題には妥協はないとしている。

Punch Line

"On issues of territory and sovereignty, China's position is firm and clear: We will not take anything that is not ours, but we will defend every inch of territory that belongs to us," Wang said.

(「領土と統治権という問題に関して、中国の態度は確固として、明瞭だ。我々は、自分たちのものでないものは奪い取らない、しかし、我々のものである領土は一寸たりとも守り抜く」と王外相は語った)

Word Check 1

(1)〜(10) の語・句の意味として最も適当なものを選択肢 (a)〜(j) の中から選びなさい。

(1) concession   (a) 譲歩
(2) defiant   (b) 認める
(3) uninhabited   (c) 人の住んでいない
(4) unreasonable   (d) 記者会見
(5) legislature   (e) 主権
(6) sovereignty   (f) 立法機関
(7) concede   (g) 評決、裁き
(8) briefing   (h) 理不尽な
(9) verdict   (i) 堅実な
(10) solid   (j) 挑戦的な

Beijing — "China will never make concessions in territorial disputes with its neighbors, while good relations with the US depend on Washington respecting Beijing's sovereignty claims," Foreign Minister Wang Yi said Saturday.

Sounding a defiant note in his first national news conference since taking office a year ago, Wang touched on disputes with Japan, the Philippines, and others that have sharpened tensions in the Asia Pacific.

China has used its coast guard to assert its claim to the entire South China Sea and its island groups and has regularly confronted Japanese patrol boats surrounding a string of uninhabited East China Sea islands controlled by Tokyo, but claimed by Beijing.

"We will never bully smaller counties, yet we will never accept unreasonable demands from smaller countries," Wang told reporters at a briefing on the sidelines of the weeklong session of the National People's Congress, China's ceremonial legislature.

"On issues of territory and sovereignty, China's position is firm and clear: We will not take anything that is not ours, but we will defend every inch of territory that belongs to us," Wang said.

Wang took a similar tough stance on Japan, although he conceded the current standoff that has sent relations to a new low was not in the interest of either party. He said that Japan, however, was solely responsible for the impasse, partly as a result of leading public figures there questioning apologies made over Tokyo's World War II aggression.

"On the two issues of principle — history and territory — there is no room for compromise. If some people in Japan insist on overturning the verdict on its past aggression, that will not be condoned by China or the world," Wang said.

While relations with the US have generally been good by comparison, Wang indicated that Beijing still felt slighted by US criticism of its human rights record, and were unresponsive to its arguments over territorial claims.

"The China-US relationship is both very important and very complex," Wang said.

"I believe that when the two sides truly respect each other's sovereignty and territorial integrity, social system and development model, core interests and major concerns, then the foundation will be a solid one," Wang said.

Structure & Writing Expression

＜見出しでは、形容詞の前の be 動詞が省略される＞
＜見出しでは、コンマは and, but などの等位接続詞の代わりに用いられる＞
＜見出しでは、コロンは say(s) の代わりに用いられ、発言者はコロンの後または前に置かれる。さらに、前文の補足説明をすることもある＞

（例）

U.S. Clark Pullout May Boost Usage of Bases in Japan: Envoy

（クラーク基地からの米軍撤退で日本の基地使用増大か、と大使）

（本文の見出し）

＊ **China (Is) Defiant on Territorial Claims (and) Demands Respect** ＜ is は省略され、コンマは and を表している＞

＊ **China's position is firm and clear: We will not take anything …**
＜コロン以下は前文 China's position is firm and clear を補足説明している＞

Comprehension

本文の内容と同じものは T、異なるものには F と答えなさい。

1. (　　) Good relations between US and China will continue if US respects China's territorial claims.
2. (　　) China only has territorial disputes with Japan.
3. (　　) China thinks relations between Japan and China are deadlocked because of Japanese politicians.
4. (　　) US questions human rights policies in China.
5. (　　) Relations between Japan and China will be smooth sailing.

Word Check 2

下線部と同じ意味となるものを記号で選びなさい。

1. China has used its coast guard to assert its claim to the <u>entire</u> South China Sea and its island groups and ...
   (a) whole (b) surrounding (c) partial

2. "We will never <u>bully</u> smaller counties, yet we will never accept unreasonable demands from smaller countries," ...
   (a) invade (b) protect (c) harass

3. Wang took a similar <u>tough</u> stance on Japan, although he conceded the current standoff that has sent relations to a new low was not in the interest of either party.
   (a) determined (b) flexible (c) difficult

4. ..., Wang indicated that Beijing still felt <u>slighted</u> by US criticism of its human rights record, and unresponsive to its arguments over territorial claims.
   (a) attacked (b) offended (c) depressed

解説

　中国、台湾、フィリピン、インドネシア、マレーシア、ベトナムに囲まれた海にスプラトリー（南沙）諸島と呼ばれる無数の島や岩礁（がんしょう）が存在している。古代から、これらの島々は東南アジ諸国及び、中国南部との重要な貿易航路に位置しており、同時に、台風などを避ける格好の島々となっていた。一時日本が領有していたが，敗戦後のサンフランシスコ平和条約で領有権を放棄した後、台湾やベトナム、フィリピンなどが実効支配していた。それが大きく変わったのが1970年代後半。この海域で海底油田の存在が確認され、その埋蔵量は200億トンともいわれる膨大な量だ。これ以降、南の楽園のような島々が宝の山となり、にわかに中国が領有権を主張して割って入った。

　中国は漁船や公船を使って盛んにこの海域を遊弋（ゆうよく）し、更には戦闘艦を派遣してベトナムなどと戦火を交え、フィリピンが実効支配しているミスチーフ諸島、スカボロー環礁などを占拠。中国漁民を住まわせるなど、既成事実を作り上げ、実効支配を狙って着々と計画を進めている。特に、スカボロー環礁はスプラトリー諸島全域の中央に位置し、この地域の支配は戦略的にきわめて重要な場所であるのみならず、フィリピンがここを失えば、領海の38％、更には50万平方キロにわたる排他的経済水域（優先的に資源を活用できる権利）を失うことになる。フィリピンにとってはこの島々の領有は死活問題となる。この記事のタイトルである"China Defiant on Territorial Claims, Demands Respect"のような中国外相の言い方は、フィリピン人留学生が言うように、「この事を日本になぞらえて言えば、けんか腰で瀬戸内海の島の領有権を主張して、言うとおりにしろ！と怒鳴りつけている」ように見えているのだ。

Unit 5
Japanese Cuisine 'Oishii'!

The Brunei Times（ブルネイ）July 5, 2007

 ## Close-up

今、ブルネイでは日本食（和食）ブーム。自分たちで食材を買い求め、家庭で和食を料理する。しかし、ブルネイの人たちがみんな和食好きとは限らない。食の文化の難しいところだ。

 ## Punch Line

> It is still considered a risky venture as the demand can change anytime, said Angela, as "not everybody is into Japanese food."

（「誰もが和食好きとは限らないし」、需要は絶えず変化するので＜和食は＞まだ危険な事業と考えられている、とアンジェラは語った）

Word Check 1

(1)～(10) の語・句の意味として最も適当なものを選択肢 (a)～(j) の中から選びなさい。

(1) ingredient   (a) 危険を冒す
(2) restock   (b) 材料、食材
(3) coincidentally   (c) 統計
(4) track down   (d) 入手可能な
(5) statistics   (e) 偶然にも
(6) demand   (f) 国民総生産
(7) risky   (g) 輸送する
(8) ship   (h) 補充する
(9) available   (i) 需要
(10) gross domestic product (j) 追跡する

25

WITH most major stores now stocking up on Japanese food products in the form of dry and frozen foods, the difficulties of obtaining the right ingredients for making a Japanese dish are now a thing of the past.

According to Assistant General Manager of Utama Grand Superstore, Cheong Hoy Loon, which has been selling Japanese food products since they opened, more and more people are now developing a taste for Japanese food. Sales were slow in the beginning, he explained, but now they're picking up.

"I think it is because more Japanese restaurants are opening," he said. "Sometimes customers want to cook similar dishes, so they buy the ingredients and cook it for themselves at home."

Pointing to a shelf arranged with a variety of sauces, he explained that there were different types of sauces for various meats.

"It's safe to say that Japanese food is healthy," he said, adding that the store restocks their supplies of Japanese food on a monthly basis.

Coincidentally, the supermarket had just added a new product to their shelves: instant soba noodles, which are less commonly seen here than the ramen-type instant noodles.

The Brunei Times tracked down their supplier Guan Hock Lee, one of the main distributors of Japanese food products in the country.

According to statistics from the Department of Economic Planning and Development, food product imports from Japan totalled $507,839 in 2005, with a slight increase of $553,332 in 2006.

"We started bringing in Japanese food products three years ago, to try to diversify our range of groceries and test the market," said Angela Sim, manager for Guan Hock Lee, which is based in Berakas.

The majority of the company's Japanese food imports are in the seafood category, such as frozen fishcakes, and are worth around $300,000 annually. Dry food imports are "limited" to $200,000 per annum.

This is because there is a higher demand for seafood, said Sim.

She explained that the products were expensive, and so were only ordered based on demand.

"If a particular product is in demand, we will order more. If overall demand is low, we will cut down," she put it simply.

Sim did agree, however, that the company had recorded a steady, albeit slow increase in demand. "At the moment, it is being well-received."

In the meantime, Guan Hock Lee has decided to play it safe with its assumptions about the local market, and still considers Japanese food products as a new thing for Bruneians.

It is still considered a risky venture as the demand can change anytime, said Angela, as "not everybody is into Japanese food."

According to Tetsuya Murase, a representative from the Department of Economic Affairs at the local Japanese Embassy, most Japanese food products in Brunei are not imported directly from Japan, but are shipped in from Singapore.

"We do not have direct flights between Japan and Brunei. Additionally, no Japanese companies want to export directly to Brunei as there are only around a hundred Japanese living in Brunei," said Murase, adding that the reluctancy also stems from high shipment costs.

"Brunei's small population does not hold much interest for a majority of food distributors," he said.

"We can buy basic Japanese products from Hua Ho and Supasave ... such as wasabi or soy sauce," said Murase.

"However, perishable products such as fruits and vegetables from Japan are not available here," he said.

However, all is not lost for Japanese food lovers in Brunei. Murase said that the Japanese government is looking into international promotion of exports, particularly fruits and vegetables, Brunei included. "Brunei's gross domestic product is very high, and is almost the same as Hong Kongs, so the Bruneian market has the means to buy expensive Japanese food," said Murase.

Structure & Writing Expression

＜重みのある前置詞や接続詞を使うと文が締まる＞

例えば、前置詞 barring（〜がなければ）は except、前置詞 pending（〜まで）は until の意味で使われる。

本文では、「…にもかかわらず、たとえ…であろうとも」という意味で albeit（接続詞）が使われている。通例省略節で使われ、although, even though の意味を持つ。

（例）

Albeit difficult, the job is getting done.

（仕事は難しそうだが、何とかなりそうだ）

本文では：**Sim did agree, however, that the company had recorded a steady, albeit slow increase in demand.** この albeit は「たとえ＜需要の伸びはゆるやか＞でも」となる。

Comprehension

本文の内容と同じものは T、異なるものには F と答えなさい。

1. (　　) With more Japanese restaurants opening, Japanese food sales have been increasing in Brunei.
2. (　　) Instant ramen noodles are more common than instant soba noodles.
3. (　　) Frozen foods are less popular than dry foods in terms of Japanese foods imports.
4. (　　) Guan Hock Lee is willing to display more types of Japanese foods.
5. (　　) More people in Brunei now purchase Japanese fruits and vegetables.

Word Check 2

下線部と同じ意味となるものを記号で選びなさい。

1. Sales were slow in the beginning, he explained, but now they're <u>picking up</u>.
   (a) worsening (b) risky (c) improving

2. "We started bringing in Japanese food products three years ago, to try to <u>diversify</u> our range of groceries and test the market," ...
   (a) decrease (b) increase (c) limit

3. She explained that the products were expensive, and so were only ordered <u>based on</u> demand.
   (a) according to (b) despite (c) in addition to

4. ... said Murase, adding that the reluctancy also <u>stems from</u> high shipment costs.
   (a) is due to (b) results in (c) adds in

解説

　日本食を世界遺産として登録するきっかけは日本人の和食離れが甚だしく、危機的状況にある事はあまり知られていない。登録を提案した一人である京都の老舗料亭の店主によると、彼の店には若い板前が日本全国から修業に集まるが、彼らが内輪で食べる賄い料理のメニューはパスタ、ハンバーグ等が圧倒的に多いと言う。これから超一流の料亭で和食を提供しようとする者達がこの状態であったため、和食の将来性に心底危機感を覚えた老舗料亭の店主たちが和食の伝統を守るために行った苦肉の策が世界文化遺産登録という手段であったわけだ。

　ところが、世界では寿司を筆頭に和食ブームが急激な勢いで広がっている。この記事にあるようにブルネイという、日本人にはあまり馴染みがない国でも和食が急速に広がりつつあり、日本食材は今後、大きなビジネスチャンスとなるようだ。ブルネイはボルネオ島にあり、石油、天然ガスが豊富。2010年の統計によるとGDPは119億ドルと、日本でいえば鳥取県の約半分の経済規模でしかない。が、エネルギー輸出が盛んなおかげで、一人当たりのGDPは28,000ドルと東南アジアの国では上位にある。しかも、豊富な資金が医療費無料、所得税ゼロなどの形で国民に還元されており、個人の購買力は相当高いのだ。

　この記事は和食の食材が少々高くとも、ブルネイではさほど高級品とは捉えられていない事を強調しているが、その原因はこの高い購買力にある。和食離れが進む日本に反比例して和食に憧れる国が多くなっていく現象を我々日本人はどう捉えればいいのか、悩むところだろう。

Unit 6
Anime Festival Brings Japan Closer to RI

The Jakarta Post（インドネシア）September 7, 2013

Close-up

インドネシアの首都、ジャカルタで開催されたアニメイベントで、日本とインドネシア両国の関係はより一層に親密になった。会場はアニメ一色、アニメ文化は日本の大きな収入源にもなっている。

Punch Line

> "Many people here wonder why we adore anime. Meanwhile in Japan, anime is a major source of income, and Japanese people are proud of anime culture," ...

(「ここの大勢の人たちは、どうしてアニメ好きなんだろう。日本では、アニメは大きな収入源であり、日本人はアニメ文化を誇りにしている」…)

Word Check 1

(1)~(10) の語・句の意味として最も適当なものを選択肢 (a)~(j) の中から選びなさい。

(1)	kick off	(a)	商品
(2)	merchandise	(b)	公務員
(3)	abbreviation	(c)	数多くの
(4)	numerous	(d)	地下
(5)	addicted	(e)	上映（すること）
(6)	civil servant	(f)	開始する
(7)	adore	(g)	地域の
(8)	basement	(h)	夢中になる
(9)	screening	(i)	大好きである
(10)	regional	(j)	省略形

30

Anime enthusiasts may find themselves enchanted during the three-day Anime Festival Asia (AFA), which kicked off at the Jakarta Convention Center (JCC) in Senayan on Friday.

The festival treated anime lovers to a variety of original anime merchandise, performances from Japanese anime singers, movie screenings, cosplay competitions, and a café experience featuring gorgeous maids and butlers.

"This year's festival is definitely bigger and more crowded than the previous event in Kemayoran last year. I am here to check out Figma and Nendo figures," Ivan Fadila, a resident of South Tangerang, told The Jakarta Post.

Figma was referring to action figures based on popular anime characters, while Nendo is an abbreviation for Nendroid, which are anime figures represented in shorter and cuter forms.

Upon entering the festival's venue, visitors were instantly exposed to numerous Figma, Nendroid and Gundam robots showered by spotlights and neatly displayed in glass boxes.

"I want to see the latest Gundam products. I have collected 70 pieces and spent around Rp 30 million [US$2,689] to Rp 40 million over the past two years," Adrian Hardy, 29, told the Post.

He said he became addicted to Gundam after getting a present from his girlfriend. Since then, he began buying imported products from the robot figure series, joining Gundam modification competitions, and even started a Gundam business.

Some visitors also made an effort to dress up in costumes depicting anime characters, which successfully attracted dozens of other visitors who asked to take pictures with them.

"I took a day off today to apply for a job as a civil servant, but after that, I decided to come here," Kurniawan, a marketing employee, told the Post.

The man who joined a community to learn about cosplay making, wore a shiny blue Thunder Knight Baron action figure costume, which took him two months to make specifically for a competition in Tangerang.

Andi Fadilla, another anime buff, said he might not have had a chance to visit Japan yet, but he was satisfied with experiencing a small taste of Japanese pop culture at the event. The fan of the One

Piece manga series said he was keen to see original merchandise at the festival, and to watch the performance of some anime singers.

"Many people here wonder why we adore anime. Meanwhile in Japan, anime is a major source of income, and Japanese people are proud of anime culture," he said.

Visitors can also buy Japanese snacks such as takoyaki (fried potato and octopus balls) and dorayaki (bean pancakes) at the basement while checking out affordable anime merchandise such as posters, postcards, key chains and pins made by local artists.

Those who want to have a fancy teatime experience served by cute butlers and maids dressed up in school uniforms have to queue to enter Atelier Royale Butler Café and Moe Moe Kyun Maid Café, which is also located in the basement.

Highlights on Saturday include movie screenings of Puella Magi Madoca Magica and Gundam Unicorn episode 6, and anime musical performances by Babymetal, fripSide and Kalafina. While on Sunday, visitors can watch the Japanese pop-rock artist TM Revolution's performance, as well as the Detective Conan movie screening, and the AFA regional cosplay championship Indonesia preliminary session.

affordable
購入しやすい

queue　列に並ぶ

Puella Magi Madoca Magica
『魔法少女まどか☆マギカ』

preliminary session
予選

Structure & Writing Expression

＜補足説明＞

メディアの記事では、読者の理解を助けるために語句や記事の背景などについて、関係詞節、同格構文、ダッシュなどを用いて補足説明をすることがある。特に登場人物の職業、肩書き、趣味などの紹介には、同格構文や関係詞節が頻繁に用いられる。

（例）

(1) ... Ivan Fadila, a resident of South Tangerang, told The Jakarta Post.

＜Ivan Fadila と a resident of South Tangerang とは同格。関係代名詞＜制限用法＞が省略されているのと同じ用法で Ivan Fadila who is a resident of South Tangerang という意味。

(2) ... Kurniawan, a marketing employee, told the Post.
（注）the Post = The Jakarta Post「ジャカルタ・ポスト紙」

(3) ... Andi Fadilla, another anime buff ...
（注）buff =…狂〔通、ファン〕（例）Ask him anything about anime; he's a big anime buff.（アニメのことなら彼に聞いてごらん，何でも知っているよ）

Comprehension

本文の内容と同じものは T、異なるものには F と答えなさい。

1. (　　) More people visited the festival this year than last year.
2. (　　) All visitors had to wear anime characters costumes.
3. (　　) A man joined the event instead of job hunting.
4. (　　) Visitors enjoy upscale Japanese foods.
5. (　　) Only anime was featured in this festival.

Word Check 2

下線部と同じ意味となるものを記号で選びなさい。

1. This year's festival is definitely bigger and more crowded than the <u>previous</u> event in Kemayoran last year.
   (a) treasured   (b) past   (c) future

2. Some visitors also <u>made an effort</u> to dress up in costumes depicting anime characters, which successfully …
   (a) hesitated   (b) appeared   (c) tried

3. He said he became <u>addicted</u> to Gundam after getting a present from his girlfriend.
   (a) affordable   (b) critical   (c) devoted

4. The fan of the One Piece manga series said he <u>was keen</u> to see original merchandise at the festival, and to watch the performance of some anime singers.
   (a) was excited   (b) criticized   (c) came

解説

　2013年9月にインドネシアで開催されたAnime Festival Asiaの賑わい振りを活写したThe Jakarta Post紙の記事。この記事の特徴は記者そのものがオタクっぽいところである。彼（彼女？）自身、日本のアニメ事情に詳しく、さらには会場で売られていた、たこ焼き、どら焼きなどの日本のジャンク・フードに興味を持っている様子が文章そのものに滲み出ていて、日本人として心が弾むような記事に仕立てられているところが何よりもうれしい。アニメ・コスプレでキメた男性や女性が会場のあちこちで一般客から記念写真を取ってくれるようにせがまれて人気者になっていく様子、ガンダムのフィギアにはまって2年間で2,500から3,000ドルと、インドネシア人の平均収入（2014年1月現在、平均月収は日本円で約2万円）からは考えられないような金額を費やして集めている29歳の男性が記事に登場。如何に現代のインドネシアが日本のサブカルチャーを受け入れているかを具体的なエピソードで綴る手法でテンポもよく、明るく、活気に満ちた会場の雰囲気がよく伝わってくる。

　世界中で、若者を中心としたカルチャー・シーンの中で日本のアニメ文化が浸透しており、この記事に採りあげられたようなフェスティバルが世界各地で開催されている事はよく知られている。それも地域の経済発展規模によって年々派手になっている。インドネシアでこのようなフェスが開催されたことはこの国の経済が発展している証拠であり、その具現化の象徴として、フィギュア集めに大金を投じられる豊かな若者が出てきたという事実こそこの記事が伝えたい事だったのではないだろうか。

Unit 7

Japan Looks to Malaysia to Globalise

The New Strait Times（マレーシア）February 6, 2014

Close-up

マレーシアは、多民族国家である。一時はマレーシア人を優先する政策があり、中国人指導によるシンガポールの独立という歴史もあるが、民族集団同士が互いの「合意」に基づき、互いの「血筋」を温存することによって、民族集団の相互間に生じる軋轢(あつれき)を解く方程式を大胆に提起し、実行していく。この過程が「内なる国際化」、つまり文化多元主義である。日本の将来を担う若者たちは、この国際化を見習い、将来に向けて構築する「国際的に通用する人材の育成」に馴染む体験を、国際社会マレーシアで習得することは必要なことだ。

Punch Line

> Japanese people are extremely homogeneous, speaking one language, thinking the same way and behaving in the same manner. They need to understand different languages, know about different religions and cultures of people from around the world. In essence, young Japanese need to "globalise."

（日本人はきわめて均一的であり、1つの言語を話し、同じように考え、同じような振る舞いをする。日本人は、世界の人々のさまざまな言語を理解し、さまざまな宗教や文化を理解する必要がある。本質的に日本の若者は「国際化される」べきだ）

Word Check 1

(1)~(10) の語・句の意味として最も適当なものを選択肢 (a)~(j) の中から選びなさい。

(1) dwindle　　　　　　　　(a) 始める
(2) launch　　　　　　　　 (b) 製造業者
(3) human resources　　　　(c) 前例がないほど
(4) homogeneous　　　　　 (d) 交渉する
(5) unprecedentedly　　　　(e) 縮小する
(6) loyalty　　　　　　　　(f) 忠誠心
(7) industrialist　　　　　　(g) 多民族の
(8) negotiate　　　　　　　(h) 単一の
(9) multiethnic　　　　　　 (i) 人材
(10) epoch-making　　　　　(j) 画期的な

35

Dr Mahathir advocated LEP (Look East Policy) soon after he took office as prime minister of Malaysia in 1981. He encouraged Malaysian students to go to Japan to become good engineers by learning the Japanese way of nation rebuilding after the world war, and to make use of this knowledge for nation building of Malaysia.

However, the Japanese economy started to dwindle from the 1990s and failed to ride the wave of globalisation of the world economy well.

Prime Minister Shinzo Abe recently launched "Abenomics with three arrows strategy" to revive the economy, and one of the challenges is how to open Japanese society and nurture young people to become "globalised human resources".

Japanese people are extremely homogeneous, speaking one language, thinking the same way and behaving in the same manner. They need to understand different languages, know about different religions and cultures of people from around the world. In essence, young Japanese need to "globalise".

After the nation's defeat in World War 2, the Japanese people rose from the rubble to restore and rebuild their country. The people showed their strength in pursuing goals to achieve a common cause.

Well-disciplined Japanese workers were unprecedentedly competitive, with a strong sense of loyalty in companies that welcomed them just like a family would, under the lifetime employment system. "Japan Inc" worked well till the end of the last century.

Although Japanese innovation succeeded in manufacturing products that attracted and satisfied world consumers, these products, with state-of-the-art technology, were aimed first at satisfying the more than 100 million Japanese citizens, rather than the different peoples of the world.

However, one symbolic case of the need for change is the Internet-linked i-mode mobile phone, introduced in Japan in 1999. It was the first and best of its kind in the world, but in the end, was sarcastically named a "Galapagos-ed product" because it was not usable outside of Japan.

Japanese industrialists had neglected new world standards established in the global market. They also paid little attention to the needs of consumers outside of Japan.

Quite belatedly today, the Japanese have started to say that we need young people who can speak foreign languages to communicate and negotiate with different peoples of the world, who understand different religions, cultures and traditions, and have a good grasp of the diverse needs of world consumers.

The Japanese government is also striving to "globalise" universities and attract foreign students by introducing classes conducted in English with visiting foreign professors. Japanese students, meanwhile, sit English proficiency tests, and are encouraged to go abroad to study and learn about different cultures and religions.

Malaysia is a multiethnic, multi-religious and multicultural society where very kind "internationalised people" welcome all. A good majority of Malaysians are multi-lingual and speak Malay, Chinese, Tamil and English fluently.

As a strong advocate of the "Look Malaysia Policy," I have been working as a "UTM distinguished ambassador" and succeeded in bringing Japanese students to study at MJIIT.

Najib recently launched the "Second Wave of Look East Policy" to help make LEP more business and research and development oriented, linked with Japanese business and state-of-the-art technology in environment, renewable energy, green technology, solid waste management, small- and medium-sized enterprises.

I wish that Malaysians and Japanese could understand the importance of this epoch-making trial in education at MJIIT as an Asian hub of higher education. I hope this trial will be successful and more Asian and Japanese students will come to study there and excel among Malaysian and international students in this multicultural society.

And when it comes to Japanese students, I hope they will become "globalised human resources," who will open up and internationalise Japanese society and contribute to revive Japan's economy.

Structure & Writing Expression

< ...when it comes to ... の to（前置詞）の後に名詞がくる >

「～となると」という意味で使われる。

（例）

When it comes to sports, you can't beat Tom.

（スポーツとなると、トムにはかなわない）

本文では：

And **when it comes to** Japanese students, I hope **they will** become "globalized human resources," ...

Comprehension

本文の内容と同じものは T、異なるものには F と答えなさい。

1. (　　) Japanese economy remains in decline because Japan couldn't ride the wave of globalization.
2. (　　) Internet-linked i-mode mobile phones were a best-selling product all over the world.
3. (　　) The Japanese government is attempting to attract foreign students by globalizing universities.
4. (　　) Malaysians should learn about globalization using Japan as an example.
5. (　　) New "LEP" targets business, and research and development.

Word Check 2

下線部と同じ意味となるものを記号で選びなさい。

1. Prime Minister Shinzo Abe recently launched "Abenomics with three arrows strategy" to revive the economy, and …
   (a) ruin　　　　　　　(b) inflate　　　　　　(c) revitalize

2. Although Japanese innovation succeeded in manufacturing products that attracted and satisfied world consumers, …
   (a) affected　　　　　(b) fascinated　　　　(c) reached

3. Japanese students, meanwhile, sit English proficiency tests, and are encouraged to go abroad to study and learn about different cultures and religions.
   (a) take　　　　　　　(b) give　　　　　　　(c) pass

4. I wish this trial will be successful and more Asian and Japanese students will come to study there and excel among Malaysian and international students in this multicultural society.
   (a) communicate with　(b) compete with　　(c) surpass

解説

　明治維新以降、アジアの国々は日本の近代化を見習おうと若者を中心に日本留学熱が高まった。例えばベトナム、ここでは後にベトナム独立運動の英雄とされるファン・ボイ・チャウが日露戦争直後に訪日、宗主国フランス駆逐のために日本からの武器供与を申し入れた。その後、彼は日本の近代化をベトナム人の若者に学ばせるために東遊運動（ドンズー運動）を起こし、密航させてまで若者を日本に送り込んだ。日露戦争勝利後は中国でも日本留学ブームが起きて、魯迅を始めとする大量の中国人の若者が日本を目指したのである。

　第二次大戦後、敗戦からの目覚ましい復興にいち早く注目したのがこの記事にあるように、マレーシアのマハチール首相だ。彼はLook East 政策（東方重視策＝日本に学べ）を積極的に進めたのである。その後日本はこの記事にあるように、技術力で国力を付け、世界第2位の経済大国にまで登り詰めた。が、市場は世界に拡散しているのにもかかわらず、その指向は日本人1億2千万人が満足する内向きな傾向となり、グローバルなダイナミズムを失って行った。その結果、終身雇用、年功序列などの弊害が目立つようになり、日本社会そのものが制度疲労を起こし、技術までもガラパゴス化してしまったのだ。

　記事ではこの状況を打開するには日本の若者がグローバル化を身をもって体験する事であり、その格好の場として多民族、多言語、多文化国家であるマレーシアがあるとしており、今度は日本がマレーシアの存在から学ぶべき時期である事を盛んに強調している。確かにその点はあるだろうが、この問題は、歴史的に多民族国家であり続けた文化と日本のような歴史と伝統を持つ単一民族の文化との根本的な違いを抜きに簡単には語れないだろう。

Unit 8
Deepening Vietnam-Japan Strategic Partnership

The Hanoitimes（ベトナム）December 16, 2013

Close-up

ベトナムのグエン・タン・ズン首相と安倍晋三首相がベトナムで会見。両首脳は両国の戦略的パートナーシップをさらに固め、深めることで一致した。両国は重要な経済的協力の実施に向けて、密なる関係を続けて行くことを誓い合った。

Punch Line

PM Dung said Vietnam always treasures cooperation with Japan, and wishes to boost a strategic partnership with the country in a more comprehensive manner.

（ベトナムは、常に日本との協力を尊重し、さらに広範囲な規模で、日本との戦略的パートナーシップを高めたい、とズン首相は語った）

Word Check 1

(1)~(10) の語・句の意味として最も適当なものを選択肢 (a)~(j) の中から選びなさい。

(1) cement		(a) 実施
(2) consolidation		(b) 優先する
(3) implementation		(c) 固める
(4) laud		(d) 好ましい
(5) competiveness		(e) 賞賛する
(6) prioritize		(f) 航行
(7) favorable		(g) 競争力
(8) navigation		(h) 署名する
(9) aviation		(i) 強化
(10) witness		(j) 飛行

Vietnamese PM Nguyen Tan Dung on December 15 (local time) held talks with his Japanese counterpart Shinzo Abe and discussed directions and a number of specific measures to further cement and deepen the Vietnam-Japan strategic partnership.

The two leaders were pleasant to witness the new progress in bilateral cooperation in all fields.

Practical activities in celebrating the Vietnam-Japan Friendship Year and the 40th anniversary of diplomatic ties have made significant contributions to the consolidation of friendship and mutual understanding between the two peoples.

PM Dung said Vietnam always treasures cooperation with Japan and wishes to boost a strategic partnership with the country in a more comprehensive manner.

The two leaders agreed on the significance of the maintenance of high-level meetings and the effective implementation of cooperation mechanisms, while lauding the setting-up of the security dialogue mechanism.

The two sides pledged to continue their close coordination in the implementation of important economic cooperation projects such as the North-South Highway, the construction of the Ninh Thuan No. 2 nuclear power plant and the Vietnam Space Centre.

Japanese Prime Minister Shinzo Abe announced an official development assistance package valued at around US$ 1 billion for Vietnam to five projects in the second half of the 2013 fiscal year.

The projects include two sections of the North-South Highway, two infrastructure development projects at Lach Huyen Port in Hai Phong city, and a program to support Vietnam in responding to climate change and enhance its competitiveness.

The Japanese side also promised to consider Vietnam's proposal to build a Vietnam-Japan friendship hospital and expand the program training Vietnamese nurses in Japan.

The two leaders also committed to considering the possibility of signing a plan of action to realize agricultural cooperation between the two countries, including the establishment of a joint working group in the field.

The Vietnamese leader affirmed that Vietnam will create all possible conditions for Japanese firms to invest in Vietnam by effectively conducting the Vietnam-Japan Joint Initiative in improving investment environment in Vietnam.

The Japanese Government chief promised to support Vietnam in carrying out action plans in six prioritized sectors included in Vietnam's industrialization strategy and the Vietnam-Japan cooperation framework by 2020 with a view to 2030.

Japan will also consider Vietnam's suggestion to create favorable condition for Vietnamese agricultural products to enter the Japanese market.

Both host and guest agreed that cooperation in human resources development is among key issues of the bilateral relationship, welcomed the initiative to establish the Vietnam-Japan University in Ha Noi and consented to jointly facilitate the project's early implementation.

The two leaders also talked international and regional issues of common concern. They agreed on the importance of ensuring peace, stability and development in the region, including peace, security, safety and freedom of navigation and aviation based on international law.

They affirmed to continue closely working at international forums, organizations, contributing to peace, stability, cooperation and prosperity in the region.

After the talks, PMs Dung and Abe witnessed the signing of a diplomatic note of exchange for three projects in the 2013 fiscal year worth 54 billion JPY, namely the international terminal T2 of Noi Bai International Airport, the Da Nhim hydro-power plant and Hanoi's belt road 3's Mai Dich-Nam Thang Long section flyover.

Ha Noi
ハノイ市、ベトナムの首都、人口650万人

belt road
環状道路

flyover
高架橋

Structure & Writing Expression

＜同一語の反復を避ける＞

同じ語を重ねて使った文章は稚拙で単調になりがちである。簡素で生き生きした文章を心がけるメディアの文体では、同一語や代名詞の反復をできるだけ避け、できる限り別の語で言い換える。

（例）

The British Broadcasting said that it was ending its new operation in India …

The publicly-owned corporation said that censorship by his government was preventing …

＜The British Broadcasting の言い換えが The publicly-owned corporation（その公社）となっている＞

本文では：

安倍晋三首相は his Japanese counterpart Shinzo Abe となっている。Vietnamese PM Nguyen Tan Dung に対するタイトルである。

- PM Dung（グエン・タン・ズン首相）
- The Vietnamese leader（グエン・タン・ズン首相）
- The Japanese Government chief（安倍晋三首相）
- Both host and guest（グエン・タン・ズン首相と安倍晋三首相）
- The two leaders（グエン・タン・ズン首相と安倍晋三首相）
- PMs Dung and Abe（グエン・タン・ズン首相と安倍晋三首相）

等々といった具合である。

Comprehension

本文の内容と同じものは T、異なるものには F と答えなさい。

1. (　　) Diplomatic ties between Vietnam and Japan have been continued for more than half a century.
2. (　　) The program for training Vietnamese nurses has already been started.
3. (　　) The Vietnamese leader wants Japanese firms to invest more in his country.
4. (　　) Two countries have anxiety in their peace.
5. (　　) Japan will spend 54 billion dollars on the infrastructure of Vietnam.

Word Check 2

下線部と同じ意味となるものを記号で選びなさい。

1. PM Dung said Vietnam always <u>treasures</u> cooperation with Japan and …
   (a) understands　　　(b) undermines　　　(c) underlines

2. The two sides <u>pledged</u> to continue their close coordination in the implementation of important economic cooperation projects such as …
   (a) paid　　　(b) promised　　　(c) declined

3. The two leaders also talked international and regional issues of common <u>concern</u>.
   (a) goal　　　(b) business　　　(c) worry

4. … exchange for three projects in the 2013 fiscal year worth 54 billion JPY, <u>namely</u> the international terminal T2 of Noi Bai International Airport, the Da Nhim hydro-power plant and Hanoi's belt road 3's Mai Dich-Nam Thang Long section flyover.
   (a) that is to say　　　(b) including　　　(c) except for

解説

　2013年末、安倍首相がベトナムを訪問、日本とベトナムの外交関係樹立40周年記念行事に参加したことを嬉々として伝えたベトナム紙の記事である。東シナ海の日中対立後、激しい反日デモなど一連の中国側が示した行動と中国経済の先行き不透明な状況に嫌気がさした日本企業が相次いで中国から撤退している。中国から出て行った企業の行き先は最近中国から距離を置き、民主化政策をとっているミャンマーと質の高い労働力を抱えたベトナムである。

　ベトナムは第2次世界大戦直後南北に分断された国となったが、旧宗主国フランスを追い出し、後にアメリカの支援を受けた南ベトナムとの戦いに北ベトナムが勝利し、統一国家となったという歴史を持っている。

　統一後のベトナムは中国と同じく社会主義国として東南アジア域内で台頭してきたが、中国は同じアジアに強力な社会主義国の誕生を喜ばず、北部国境地帯から中国軍が攻め入り、中越戦争が起きた。ベトナムは米軍が残した最新鋭の武器を駆使して中国軍を撃退したが、これ以降、改革開放経済体制（ドイモイ体制）に切り替え、米国を始め、西側世界と交流し、著しい経済成長を遂げた。経済発展を遂げているベトナムにとっては日本企業の中国撤退はそれの受け皿としてさらなる発展の糧とするチャンスと見えているのだ。

　記事にもあるように日本からの巨額の投資は経済的な日越連携を強化、更に、スプラトリー諸島・パラセル諸島領有問題で中国と争っているベトナムにとって、日本と共同歩調を採って海上交通の自由と安全を保証する事が対中国戦略上重要事項となる。だからこそ、この記事はタイトルにもあるように、日越の戦略的関係の深化をたたえる表現になっていると言えよう。

Unit 9
Asia's Deep Wounds of War Need German-style Healing (1)

The Nation（タイ）March 11, 2014

Close-up

中国やその他の国が、日本に歴史の償いをさせようとしているが、それは、平和的な解決には至らないだろう。一方、過去の残忍な行為に対するドイツの悔恨(かいこん)に対して、中国は賛同を表明している。

Punch Line

The sooner China and other Asian countries stop browbeating Japan with the German model, the better everyone would be: The German example remains theoretically relevant, but is of no practical application to Japan and its neighbours.

（中国およびその他のアジア諸国が、ドイツをモデルとした場合と同様に、日本たたきを止めるや否や、誰もがより好ましい状態になるであろう。だけど、ドイツの場合は論理の筋が通っていると思われているが、だからといって、それを日本また隣国に実践的適用はできない）

Word Check 1

(1)～(10) の語・句の意味として最も適当なものを選択肢 (a)～(j) の中から選びなさい。

(1) ingenuity
(2) routinely
(3) corner
(4) atonement
(5) law-abiding
(6) instinctively
(7) tasteless
(8) afflict
(9) relevant
(10) reconciliation

(a) 本能的に
(b) 日常的に
(c) 苦しめる
(d) 関連のある
(e) 巧妙さ
(f) 和解
(g) 遵法(じゅんぽう)の
(h) 追い込む
(i) 悪趣味な
(j) 償(つぐな)い

Diplomats are paid to dream up clever ways of promoting their country's interests. But occasionally, diplomatic ingenuity can go too far, as a team of Chinese diplomats tasked with planning President Xi Jinping's forthcoming visit to Germany recently discovered.

Beijing offered to set aside a big chunk of President Xi's visit to commemorative events praising the way Germany dealt with its historic responsibility for World War II. Chinese officials assumed that this would please their German hosts, for the manner by which Germany routinely expresses remorse for the murderous deeds of its past is rightly and universally admired.

Yet to Beijing's surprise, the Germans flatly turned down most of these proposals, realising that China's real aim was not to engage in a search for historic truths, but rather, to make negative comparisons between the German model of contrition and the alleged absence of historic remorse in Japan.

This obscure diplomatic tussle, conducted away from the media's gaze, will soon be forgotten. But the episode should serve as a warning to Chinese officials that their frequent efforts to corner Japan because of the country's lack of historic atonement, are sometimes misguided.

Those who think that Germany could ever be the ideal place to criticise other countries for failing to live up to their historic responsibility are guilty of a fundamental misunderstanding of the German experience.

The German Experience

Germans see their atonement not as a national, but as a deeply personal one: The TV dramas which attract the biggest audiences in the country are those which show how ordinary, humane and otherwise law-abiding Germans during the 1940s either turned a blind eye to the mass murders committed in their midst, or even took part in them.

German politicians continue to use every opportunity to apologise to other nations for what their country did. But the most powerful German apology ever issued to the world was accomplished without actually saying a single word: It came in 1970, when then German Chancellor Willy Brandt fell to his knees before a memorial commemorating the hundreds of thousands of people butchered by the Nazis in Warsaw, Poland.

The act, now remembered as the "Warsaw Genuflection," could have easily been dismissed as just cheap propaganda, a meaningless photo opportunity. But millions of Europeans were moved to tears by the gesture, precisely because they instinctively understood that it was the product of Germany's internal moral cleansing.

Because they view their experience as unique, and because they engage in acts of historic atonement not to please outsiders, but to deal with their own personal sense of guilt, the Germans have never regarded their model as exportable. Therefore, the suggestion that Germany should now teach Japan a lesson in historic contrition is seen as both irrelevant and tasteless. It's akin to asking someone who has succeeded in coming to terms with his own emotional and psychological traumas to go out and preach to other people who may be afflicted.

The sooner China and other Asian countries stop browbeating Japan with the German model, the better everyone would be: The German example remains theoretically relevant, but is of no practical application to Japan and its neighbours.

Still, there are other aspects of Germany's historic atonement which are worth copying if a historic reconciliation between Japan and past war victims is ever to become a reality. The first is the principle that achieving such a historic "closure" requires a concentration on the key bones of historic contention, rather than on every little dispute from a controversial past.

(To be continued.)

Structure & Writing Expression

＜メディア特有の語・句＞

簡潔な表現を求めるメディアの記事では、分詞を最大限に活用する。特に名詞の前につく分詞にメディア特有の語・句があるので、早く馴れることが大切である。

（例）

the **alleged** improper payment（いわゆる不正支払い）

the **attempted** coup（クーデター未遂）

the **continued** space research（宇宙調査の継続）

his **planned** visit to Moscow（彼のモスクワ訪問計画）

a **proposed** amendment（修正提案）

his **purported** kidnapping（彼が誘拐されたという事件）

the new **stepped-up** raids（新たな攻撃強化）

本文では：

...and the **alleged** absence of historic remorse in Japan.

Comprehension

本文の内容と同じものはT、異なるものにはFと答えなさい。

1. (　　) President Xi Jinping's visit succeeded as Chinese diplomats had planned.
2. (　　) Germans dislike TV dramas which depict the mass murders which took place in the 1940s.
3. (　　) Europeans forgave the Germans when a German leader fell to his knees in front of a memorial.
4. (　　) Many Germans believe Germany should teach Japan a lesson in war contrition.
5. (　　) There are some aspects which we should learn from Germany in regard to reconciliation.

Word Check 2

下線部と同じ意味となるものを記号で選びなさい。

1. Beijing offered to set aside a big <u>chunk</u> of President Xi's visit to commemorative events praising the way Germany dealt with its historic responsibility for World War II.
   (a) connection   (b) importance   (c) part

2. ... that their frequent efforts to corner Japan because of the country's lack of historic atonement, are sometimes <u>misguided</u>.
   (a) misunderstood   (b) useless   (c) unwise

3. The act, now remembered as the "Warsaw Genuflection," could have easily been <u>dismissed</u> as just cheap propaganda, a meaningless photo opportunity.
   (a) ignored   (b) respected   (c) admired

4. Because they view their experience as <u>unique</u>, and because they engage in acts of historic atonement not to please outsiders, but to deal with their own personal sense of guilt, ...
   (a) strange   (b) individual   (c) mutual

解 説

　中国や韓国の首脳が相次いでドイツを訪問し、第二次世界大戦での敗戦国であるドイツの戦後処理を褒めたたえ、日本の敗戦処理が如何に間違っているかを際立たせる戦略を推進している。このような状態に対して、タイ紙がヨーロッパとドイツの歴史と、アジア諸国と日本、特に中国と韓国との関係史を比較。更には日独両国は同じ敗戦国でありながら、両国民の間には歴史認識の違いがあり、それを十分理解していないと誤解を生み、ことさら日本を謝罪のみで追い詰めようとする事では決して平和を導き出せないと、実に冷静で知的な筆さばきで主張している。

　この記事では中国の習近平主席が訪独に際して行った上記のような趣旨での演説に対してドイツが迷惑そうな態度を見せた事。その理由として、中国の本当の目的は歴史的事実を探究する事ではなく、日本と中国の歴史認識問題にドイツを巻き込む事にあったからだとしている。ドイツ人は第二次大戦で起きた事に対する贖罪は国家としてではなく、きわめて個人的な事柄だと見ている。習近平氏も採り上げてドイツを絶賛した、1970年にポーランドを訪問した時の西独首相ブラント氏がユダヤ人強制収容所の前で跪き、涙したというエピソードはあくまでもブラント氏の個人的な行為であると断じている。事実、ドイツはユダヤ人に対しては賠償金を支払っているが、戦争相手国には国家としての謝罪もせず、賠償金は一銭も払ってはいないのだ。

　実を言うと、贖罪を個人的な事柄とするのは、ドイツの戦後処理と深い関わりがある。ヒトラーはナチス党を合法的な選挙で政権党にした。従って、ナチスの政策はドイツ国民の総意という事になる。しかし後のニュルンベルグ裁判でユダヤ人虐殺が国策として行われていた事が明らかにされた。この事に対してドイツ人は全く知らされていなかった、よって虐殺行為自体は当時の政府であるナチスに責任があるが、それを知らなかった個々のドイツ人にも責任があるとして、1985年に時の大統領ワイツゼッカー氏が戦後40年を記念してドイツ議会でその趣旨の演説を行った。ドイツ人の間では戦後、この歴史認識が定着しているのである。この記事の前半は上記のようなドイツの戦後処理とそれを可能にしたドイツ人の歴史認識にまで踏み込んだ上での記述となっており、日本のメディアではほとんど目にできない秀でた内容のものになっている。

Unit 10
Asia's Deep Wounds of War Need German-style Healing (2)

The Nation（タイ）March 11, 2014

🌐 Close-up

歴史的事実は取り替えが効かない。しかし、政治家が、自分たちに、ことを有利に導けば、さしたる難しいことでもない。日本の場合の損害賠償は、直ぐにはこうも行きそうもない。このように考慮すると、日本を歴史的責任から解き放つことは至難だ。ドイツの場合の贖罪は、より優れた将来を探し求めて困惑した過去を取り除く責任を分かち合うため、個人、国家として集団で最良の「施策」が行使されたのである。残念なことに、今日のアジアではこの例は適用されない。

🌐 Punch Line

> If a Japanese prime minister were to set fire to the Yasukuni shrine, go to Nanjing to fall on his knees in contrition for the crime perpetrated against China, and then fly to Seoul to embrace the few surviving Korean wartime sex slaves, would this be the end of the story?

（もし日本の首相が靖国神社に火を放ち、中国に犯した罪をあがなうため、南京に出向いてひざまずくなら、さらにはソウルに飛び、存命中の従軍慰安婦を抱擁するならば、それで話は済んだというのか？）

🌐 Word Check 1

(1)~(10) の語・句の意味として最も適当なものを選択肢 (a)~(j) の中から選びなさい。

(1) reparation　　　　(a) 抗議
(2) reinstate　　　　 (b) 無差別な
(3) outcry　　　　　 (c) 元に戻す
(4) evocative　　　　(d) 消える
(5) tangled　　　　　(e) 繁栄
(6) indiscriminate　　(f) 思い出させる
(7) perish　　　　　 (g) 説得力がある
(8) compelling　　　 (h) もつれた
(9) prosperity　　　　(i) 免除する
(10) absolve　　　　 (j) 賠償

In the case of Europe, Germany's neighbours gave up any demands for reparations at the end of World War II; money was paid to individual victims, but not to governments.

Nobody told the new German government how to behave. And, although some European governments gulped, nobody complained when the Germans kept the same melody for their national anthem as they had during Hitler's days, and reinstated more or less the same historic insignia for the German military; complete with midnight torchlight ceremonies, which many of Germany's neighbours used to regard as sinister.

Every single one of these episodes could have resulted in a European outcry similar to that over Japan's Yasukuni shrine, but they did not, because European governments understood that the Germans needed to concentrate on dealing with the biggest and most evocative of the war crimes—the Holocaust.

In the case of Japan, however, almost every single historic dispute is now put forward as being of equal importance, requiring an urgent response from Tokyo. The Japanese are expected to offer apologies for the occupation of Korea, and contrition for the invasion of China.

They are also asked to atone for the Nanjing Massacre, and accept the tally of the victims butchered there, as well as address the question of Korea's so-called "comfort women," compensation for forced labourers, a variety of territorial disputes, plus issues such as the question of names given to bodies of water surrounding Japan. Even a politically brave and well-meaning future Japanese prime minister would not know where to begin if he wanted to deal with this tangled web of historic demands.

Every Nation Has a Role

Another lesson from Germany worth remembering is that reconciliation works best when it engages everyone. Although Nazi Germany conceived and unleashed the Holocaust, many European governments now admit that through omission or commission, they also bear some responsibility for mass murder.

Historians in France and Britain are also debating whether the indiscriminate carpet-bombing of German cities during the war was a crime which requires a profound apology.

All of this has allowed Germany to cope with its horrible past in an easier manner: The burden placed by the heavy hand of history was at least partially shared with its neighbours.

And the same could happen with Japan as well. If the Chinese government was prepared to address the painful history of the millions of Chinese who perished in political purges and famines over the past six decades, as well as of the hundreds of thousands who died unnecessarily during World War II due to poor and politically divided Chinese military leadership, Beijing would have a far more powerful case against Japan.

The same applies to South Korea: If President Park Geun-hye was prepared to show even a fraction of the zeal she puts into demanding apologies from Tokyo towards an examination of how many people died during her father's iron rule, her stance on Japan would be even more compelling. The message from Europe is that it's possible to shame nations into coming to terms with their past. And the best way of doing so is by example: Those with a clean conscience have every right to demand nothing less from others.

But the most important lesson from the experience of Germany's example is that, in return for contrition, Germany was offered security, prosperity and full membership in the European community of nations. Germany now leads Europe in every respect and, although many of its neighbours are not particularly fond of this outcome, they accept that it is the result of German hard work and success, rather than some malevolent plot to take over the continent. The reconciliation is therefore complete.

Japan's Responsibilities

But what is Japan being offered now in return for its atonement? If a Japanese prime minister were to set fire to the Yasukuni shrine, go to Nanjing to fall on his knees in contrition for the crimes perpetrated against China, and then fly to Seoul to embrace the few surviving Korean wartime sex slaves, would this be the end of the story? Would Japan become a friend of South Korea and China? Would the territorial disputes be over? The answers are far too obvious to need spelling out. Historic truths cannot be traded, but they are easier to face if politicians see an advantage. Yet in the case of Japan, no such compensations are in the offing.

　None of these considerations absolves Japan of its historic responsibilities. But they should serve as a reminder that, just as in the case of Germany, atonement is an exercise best performed in a group, by people and nations who truly share a commitment to exorcise their troubled past in search of a better future.

　Sadly, that's not the case in today's Asia.

in the offing　近い将来に

exorcise　追い払う

Structure & Writing Expression

＜前置詞 plus の用法＞

「〜に加えて、とともに」を意味する plus は前置詞で have wealth plus ability（富も能力も持ち合わせる）といった具合に使う。

（例）Five plus nine is fourteen (5+9=14).

本文では：..., a variety of territorial disputes **plus** issues such as the question of names given to seas around Japan.

Comprehension

本文の内容と同じものは T、異なるものには F と答えなさい。

1. (　　) The European countries think that Germany should tackle only the Holocaust issue.
2. (　　) Japan should concentrate on the Nanjing Massacre.
3. (　　) The Chinese government has reflected on the political purges and famines in the country over the past sixty years.
4. (　　) Reconciliation works best when it engages everyone.
5. (　　) If the Prime Minister of Japan copes with each issue properly, Japan will become friends with its neighboring countries.

Word Check 2

下線部と同じ意味となるものを記号で選びなさい。

1. In the case of Japan, however, almost every single historic dispute is now put forward as being of equal importance, requiring an urgent response from Tokyo.
   (a) remembered (b) considered (c) called

2. Although Nazi Germany conceived and unleashed the Holocaust, many European governments now admit that ...
   (a) stopped (b) admitted (c) caused

3. If the Chinese government was prepared to address the painful history of the millions of Chinese who perished in political purges and famines ...
   (a) deal with (b) perish (c) remember

4. The answers are far too obvious to need spelling out.
   (a) calling out (b) explaining (c) understanding

解説

　記事の後半部分は戦後の新しいドイツに対する周辺国の基本態度に言及。結論を先に言えば、日本の周辺国のそれとの違いを比較し、アジア的現状を嘆（なげ）くという流れになっている。この記事の後半部で最初に挙げているのが新生ドイツ国歌がナチス時代と同じ楽曲である事と、戦争中と同じ様式を持った軍隊を設立したことに対してヨーロッパ各国が一切反対しなかった事実である。この事実をふまえたうえでの記事の主旨はこうだ。ヨーロッパ諸国も日本の靖国神社に対するのと同じような批判は持っているが、ドイツの戦争犯罪の中でも最優先で贖罪すべきはホロコーストに対するものである。従って、その他の事には拘（こだわ）らない。それに比較して日本では個々の歴史問題が同じように取りざたされて謝罪を求められる。この状態では日本の首相はよりよい未来のためにどの局面から始めたらよいのか分からなくなってしまう。そして、こう記述する、ナチス・ドイツ、日本、を含めてどの国にも歴史の暗部は存在している。英仏も戦争中非戦闘員を大量に殺したドイツ国内への絨毯（じゅうたん）爆撃も論争の種となっているし、中国でも戦争中に数十万人が虐殺されたと言うのならそれを許してしまった中国軍指導者の問題、戦後においても60年の間に起きた政治的な争いの中で出た数百万人の犠牲はどうなるのか。韓国でも、パク大統領の父親が大統領時代に実施した弾圧で死亡した数多くの犠牲者がいる。

　記事の最後の部分では、日本の首相が靖国神社に火を放ち、南京虐殺記念館の前で跪き、その後ソウルに飛んで存命中の従軍慰安婦を抱きしめれば謝罪は終わるのだろうか…と言う根本的な問いかけがあり、よりよい未来のために国家と国民同士が過去の問題に互いに真摯（しんし）に向き合う事がドイツの例を生かす方法だろうとする。が、最後に Sadly, that's not the case in today's Asia. と結んでいる。この最後の文を我々はどう解釈し、解決に結び付けられるのか…？

Unit 11

Japan on Backfoot in Global PR War with China after Abe Shrine Visit (1)

The Irrawaddy（ミャンマー）February 13, 2014

Close-up

安倍首相の靖国神社参拝が中国との関係を一層に悪化させ、日中宣伝合戦を煽っている。中国は日本を「悪役」と決めつけているようだ。

Punch Line

> Abe's Yasukuni Shrine visit "gave China the opportunity ... to attack Japan and send the message that China is the good guy and Japan is the bad guy."

（安倍首相の靖国神社参拝は、「中国に日本を攻撃し、中国は善人であり、日本は悪人だ、という口実を中国に与えることになった」）

Word Check 1

(1)~(10) の語・句の意味として最も適当なものを選択肢 (a)~(j) の中から選びなさい。

(1)	chill	(a)	冷え込む
(2)	dispute	(b)	論争（する）
(3)	sway	(c)	有罪判決をする
(4)	militarism	(d)	はね返り、反発
(5)	convict	(e)	根拠のない
(6)	assertiveness	(f)	揺さぶる
(7)	backlash	(g)	誓う
(8)	pledge	(h)	自己主張（の強さ）
(9)	rebuttal	(i)	反論
(10)	ungrounded	(j)	軍国主義

TOKYO/BEIJING — Japan risks losing a global PR battle with China after Prime Minister Shinzo Abe's visit to the controversial Yasukuni Shrine honoring WWII dead, and comments by other prominent figures on the wartime past helped Beijing paint Tokyo as the villain of Asia.

Sino-Japanese ties have long been plagued by territorial rows, regional rivalry, and disputes stemming from China's bitter memories of Japan's occupation of parts of the country before and during World War Two. Relations chilled markedly after a feud over the disputed East China Sea islands flared in 2012.

Beijing, however, has stepped up its campaign to sway international public opinion since Abe's Dec. 26 visit to Tokyo's Yasukuni Shrine. The shrine is seen by critics as a symbol of Japan's past militarism, because it honors leaders convicted as war criminals, along with millions of war dead.

That strategy has helped China shift some of the debate away from its growing military assertiveness in Asia, including double-digit defense spending increases, and the recent creation of an air defense identification zone in the East China Sea that was condemned by Tokyo and Washington, experts said.

"Right now, this is a real war," said Shin Tanaka, president of the Fleishman Hillard Japan Group in Tokyo, a communications consultancy firm.

"Japan and China are using missiles called 'messages,' and the reality is that a lot of damage is already happening in both countries," he added, warning of a mutual backlash of nationalist emotions and potential harm to business ties between the countries.

Abe has repeatedly said he did not visit the shrine to honor war criminals, but to pay his respects to those who died for their country, and pledge Japan would never again go to war.

Getting that message across is not easy, communications and political experts said. Abe's Yasukuni Shrine visit "gave China the opportunity ... to attack Japan and send the message that China is the good guy and Japan is the bad guy," Tanaka said.

'Goebbelsian PR Binge'

Some Japanese diplomats and officials dismissed any suggestion they were worried, saying Tokyo's rebuttals and the country's post-war record of peace would win the day.

"Their Goebbelsian PR binge – repeat it 100 times then it becomes true, ungrounded or not – shows all the symptoms of a Leninist regime still remaining in the 21st century," Tomohiko Taniguchi, a councilor in the cabinet secretariat of the prime minister's office, said in an email.

He was referring to Joseph Goebbels, Adolf Hitler's minister of propaganda who held office from 1933-1945.

"Yes we feel annoyed, but the next moment we relax for we have nothing to be ashamed of."

Still, experts said Abe's shrine visit had made it easier for Beijing to try to link Abe's plans to bolster the military, and loosen limits on the pacifist constitution to Japan's militarist past.

(To be continued.)

Goebbelsian ゲッベルスの

binge 飲み騒ぎ、過度にすること

win the day 成功する

Leninist レーニン主義者（レーニンはロシアの共産主義指導者、1870-1924）

councilor in the cabinet secretariat 内閣官房内閣審議官

pacifist constitution 平和憲法

Structure & Writing Expression

<The fact is that ... の構文 >

メディア関係の文体の一つ。The hope is that ..., First impressions are that ... のように that-clause を補語に用いた S+be+that-clause の構文が好んで用いられる。なお、that-clause を導く接続詞 that はコンマになったり、時には省略されることもある。

（例） **Their argument is that** firing the first shot would be a serious departure from alliance principles.

本文では "...**the reality is that** a lot of damage is already happening in both countries," となっている。

Comprehension

本文の内容と同じものは T、異なるものには F と答えなさい。

1. (　　) Although the relationships between China and Japan were favorable, they deteriorated because of Abe's Yasukuni Shrine visit on December 26, 2013.
2. (　　) The defense budget of China increased twofold compared to one year ago.
3. (　　) Abe's Yasukuni Shrine visit helped China to feel superior to Japan.
4. (　　) Most Japanese diplomats and officials are worried because of Abe's visit to Yasukuni Shrine.
5. (　　) Taniguchi concluded that China's strategy was similar to that of Goebbels'.

Word Check 2

下線部と同じ意味となるものを記号で選びなさい。

1. Beijing, however, has <u>stepped up</u> its campaign to sway international public opinion since Abe's Dec. 26 visit to Tokyo's Yasukuni Shrine.
   (a) intensified　　　(b) begun　　　(c) held up

2. … an air defense identification zone in the East China Sea that was <u>condemned</u> by Tokyo and Washington, experts said.
   (a) approved　　　(b) announced　　　(c) denounced

3. Some Japanese diplomats and officials dismissed any suggestion they were worried, saying Tokyo's rebuttals and the country's post-war record of peace would <u>win the day</u>.
   (a) be postponed　　　(b) continue　　　(c) succeed

4. "Yes we feel <u>annoyed</u>, but the next moment we relax for we have nothing to be ashamed of."
   (a) irritated　　　(b) excited　　　(c) astonished

解説

　長期に亘って中国の援助を受け、強圧的な軍事政権を維持してきたミャンマーがようやくその頸木から脱し、民主的な政治・経済体制が採れるようになった。言わば、中国の手の内を知るこの国の新聞が現在展開中の日本と中国のプロパガンダ競争について論評している。この記事の特徴は日中のその分野に於ける争いを「戦争」と位置づけ、勝つか負けるかを注視している点だろう。

　実を言うと、一般の日本人の中には、この記事が言うように互いが敵とみなして言葉のミサイルを射ち合っているという感覚はない。従って、この国の経験に基づいた貴重な知見を示していると我々は見た方がよいだろう。

　この視点に立てば、2013年暮れの安倍首相の靖国参拝は日本をアジアの悪漢として描きたい中国政府にとっては格好の材料となる。この記事が言うように、靖国参拝は軍事費を2倍にし、東シナ海で防空識別圏を設置するなど、アジア各地域で軍事攻勢をかけている中国の問題から世界の目を逸らさせることになった。

　安倍首相は、靖国参拝は戦没者に対して不戦の誓いをする事であり、世界中の戦没者に鎮魂の情を表明した。国の命令で死亡した英霊を慰撫するのは一国の指導者としては当然の事だ…と繰り返すが、このメッセージは世界中に理解されたとは言い難く、中国に利用されてしまったのはこの記事の言う通りだろう。そして、ナチス・ドイツの宣伝相ゲッベルスのプロパガンダ手法である「100回繰り返せば不確実であろうとなかろうと、それは真実になってしまう」を引き合いに出し、中国が現在宣伝戦に於いては優位に立っている事をこの記事は示唆しているのだ。

Unit 12

Japan on Backfoot in Global PR War with China after Abe Shrine Visit (2)

The Irrawaddy（ミャンマー） February 13, 2014

Close-up

中国の駐英大使は、日本を「ハリーポッター」の悪人に例えた。日本は中国との宣伝合戦で後手にまわっている。日中関係をさらに悪化させるものに愛国心を助長するような教科書の書き換え等の問題がある。これは愛国心を煽り、火に油を注ぐものと思われる。

Punch Line

"A lie is repeated so that people are brainwashed and start to believe it."

(「嘘も繰りかえされると、洗脳され、本当のことのように思い始めるものだ」)

Word Check 1

(1)~(10) の語・句の意味として最も適当なものを選択肢 (a)~(j) の中から選びなさい。

(1) assert　　　　　　　(a) 指名された人
(2) blur　　　　　　　　(b) 指針
(3) euphemism　　　　 (c) 婉曲語法、遠まわし表現
(4) appointee　　　　　 (d) 大使
(5) ambassador　　　　 (e) 受け身の
(6) colonization　　　　(f) 自責の念
(7) villain　　　　　　　(g) ぼやけさせる、汚す
(8) remorse　　　　　　(h) 植民地化
(9) reactive　　　　　　(i) 悪人
(10) agenda　　　　　　(j) 断言する

"The most fundamental thing China asserts is that Japan is going on a path of militarism a la the 1930s. That's just nonsense," said Daniel Sneider, associate director for research at Stanford University's Shorenstein Asia-Pacific Research Center. "But the problem is the Chinese are able to blur a lot of this stuff because of what Abe did."

Recent remarks about Japan's wartime past by the chairman of NHK Japan's public broadcasting corporation and members of its board of governors have added grist to China's PR mill.

Among those remarks were comments by new NHK Chairman Katsuto Momii, who told a news conference last month that "comfort women" – a euphemism for women forced to work in Japanese wartime military brothels – had counterparts in every country at war at that time. He later apologized.

NHK's chairman is selected by a board of governors that includes four Abe appointees.

Since the start of the year, Chinese ambassadors and other officials have targeted Japan 69 times in media around the world, Japan's Foreign Ministry said. The campaign includes interviews, written commentaries and news conferences.

As of Monday, Japan had issued rebuttals in 67 cases with the other two under review, Foreign Ministry spokesman Masaru Sato said.

Asked if China had won over international opinion, Chinese Foreign Ministry spokeswoman Hua Chunying said countries such as South Korea – where memories of Japan's 1910-1945 colonization run deep – had also criticized Tokyo.

"The mistaken ways of the Japanese leader have incurred the strong opposition of the international community," Hua told reporters. "China is willing to work with other victims of the war and the international community to uphold historical justice."

Voldemort Duel

The verbal jousting has spanned the globe from capitals such as London and Washington, to remote Fiji and South Sudan.

The best known exchanges are the "Voldemort attacks," in which China's ambassador to Britain, Liu Xiaoming, last month compared Japan to the villain in the Harry Potter children's book series. In reply, Japan's envoy, Keiichi Hayashi, said China risked becoming "Asia's Voldemort".

"We try to explain that Japan faces its history squarely, and has expressed remorse ... and that Japan will continue to pursue the path of a peace-loving country," Sato said.

"Sometimes they try to link the visit to the shrine to security policy. That is a totally unrelated matter."

Still, some in Japan fear that China's PR blitz is having an impact on world opinion.

"A lie is repeated so that people are brainwashed and start to believe it," Akira Sato, head of the ruling Liberal Democratic Party's panel on defense policy, told Reuters.

Echoed a Western diplomat in Beijing: "China is being successful at getting its message across, while Japan keeps saying stupid things like questioning the existence of comfort women. I think China has changed opinions."

Tokyo's mostly reactive approach, some PR experts said, was not enough to sway international public opinion; a worry some Japanese diplomats share privately.

"Japan is very worried that China is winning this propaganda war," said an Asian diplomat based in Beijing. "Their diplomats have been asking how they can better put their side of the story, and win people in the West over."

That could be tough if Abe declines to say whether he will visit Yasukuni Shrine again, or other prominent Japanese figures make controversial comments on wartime history, experts said.

Other matters such as planned changes to Japanese textbooks to promote patriotism, could add fuel to the fire.

"Even if he doesn't go to Yasukuni Shrine again, there are plenty of issues on their (the Japanese government's) agenda," Sneider said.

🌐 Structure & Writing Expression

<挿入節の働き>

メディアでは、記者の文章と発信者の言葉をはっきり区別しておく必要がある。そのため **What Mr. A says** とか **it is said** 型の挿入節が多用される。さらに念を入れて発言者の言葉を引用符で囲むこともある。

(例)

He appealed to the Russian parliament for support for his radical policies against **what he said** was an array of conservative bureaucrats and mafia-like forces.

(彼はロシア最高会議に対して、彼の言う保守的官僚集団やマフィア勢力に対抗し、彼の基本政策を支持するように訴えた)

本文では："The most fundamental thing **they say** is to assert that Japan is going on a path of militarism a la the 1930s..."

🌐 Comprehension

本文の内容と同じものはT、異なるものにはFと答えなさい。

1. (　) Momii's remark about comfort women spurred China to criticize Japan.
2. (　) China didn't intend to attack Japan together with South Korea.
3. (　) So far China could not win over international opinion.
4. (　) Japan's reactive approach should change.
5. (　) If Abe doesn't go to Yasukuni Shrine again, relations will improve.

Word Check 2

下線部と同じ意味となるものを記号で選びなさい。

1. "But the problem is the Chinese are able to <u>blur</u> a lot of this stuff because of what Abe did."
   (a) obscure   (b) deny   (c) assert

2. "China is willing to work with other victims of the war and the international community to <u>uphold</u> historical justice."
   (a) lift   (b) strengthen   (c) maintain

3. Still, some in Japan <u>fear</u> that China's PR blitz is having an impact on world opinion.
   (a) are disappointed (b) are afraid   (c) are sorry

4. Other matters such as <u>planned</u> changes to Japanese textbooks to promote patriotism, could add fuel to the fire.
   (a) scheduled   (b) enlarged   (c) increased

解説

　この記事の後半部分は現在展開されている中国側の具体的な宣伝戦略について実例を挙げつつ解説する。それによると、中国の基本戦略は日本を1930年代のような軍国主義国家の道を歩んでいると決めつける事だとのスタンフォード大学研究者のコメントを引用。その具体例として2014年初頭から全世界の中国大使や政府要員が2月半ばまで実に69回に及ぶ記者会見や新聞寄稿原稿、インタビュー等で日本を標的にした事を挙げた。中でも最も効果的と思われるのは、駐英国中国大使が日本をハリー・ポッターの悪役に見立てた事だ。

　これら一連の中国の攻撃に対する日本の反撃は国際世論を揺るがすには不十分だとの判断を示し、中国がこの戦争に勝利しつつある現状を打開できるかどうかについて疑問を呈し、日本には靖国問題も含めて教科書問題など、中国にとってはうまく利用できる宣伝材料がまだ数多い事をこの記事では述べている。

　いずれにしても、日本人はこの記事にあるように、中国と戦争をしているという考えは全くないだろう。その事が、中国の国際世論操作による不利益として我々に降りかかってくる…！？

Unit 13

Japanese Ear Surgery 3-Day Camp Concludes

The Kuensel（ブータン）October 16, 2013

🌐 Close-up

日本の耳鼻咽喉科医療チームがブータンで医療活動に従事、手術は成功した。2011年の東日本大震災に対する祈願のお礼として、またブータン国王の日本訪問への感謝を表すために、医療活動は行われた。

🌐 Punch Line

"I'm beginning to hear in both the ears," the Thimphu thromde engineer said, after coming out of the operation room.

（手術室から出てきたそのティンプー地区工兵指揮官は、「両耳が聞こえだした」と語った）

🌐 Word Check 1

(1)~(10) の語・句の意味として最も適当なものを選択肢 (a)~(j) の中から選びなさい。

(1) painkiller   (a) 資金提供する
(2) infection   (b) 痛み止め
(3) patient   (c) 鼓膜
(4) surgeon   (d) 診断
(5) camp   (e) 感染症
(6) sponsor   (f) 出張、遠征
(7) eardrum   (g) 外科医
(8) appreciation   (h) 患者
(9) diagnosis   (i) 熟練の
(10) well-experienced   (j) 感謝

ENT: Teknath Karari calls himself a good listener. But with one of his ears blocked since college days, listening to people has always been dfficult.

But yesterday, after less than an hour in the operation room, Teknath bid goodbye to the countless antibiotic tablets and painkillers that he used to suppress pain. "I'm beginning to hear in both the ears," the Thimphu thromde engineer said, after coming out of the operation room.

Even an operation in India made possible with contributions from friends failed to correct the damage. "I still kept suffering from infections quite frequently, despite putting cotton in my ear all the time," Teknath said, recalling the agonising infections he suffered from raindrops getting into his ear while on site visits in Trongsa as district engineer.

"I had to request for a transfer to Thimphu because I couldn't obtain treatment in Trongsa," he said.

Teknath is among 25 patients operated by a group of ear nose throat (ENT) surgeons and nurses from Japan during a three-day "ear surgery camp" in Thimphu, which ends today.

The camp, sponsored entirely by personal voluntary contributions from team members, spends about USD 100 per patient for the Fibrin glue that is used to treat holes in the eardrums.

The team consists of four senior surgeons; two from Sendai ear surgi-centre (SES) and one each from Yamamoto ear surgi-centre, and Niigata University as well as two nurses from SES.

Team leader Dr Ryo Yuasa from Sendai ear surgi-centre said: "It's in return for the Bhutanese people's prayers for us after the tsunami in 2011, and also as a token of appreciation for the Bhutan royal visit to our country."

He also gifted an operation microscope, including transportation costs, the value of which is roughly USD 10,000.

Dr Yuasa, who is on his second visit to the country, invented the Fibrin glue technique to fix the eardrum.

He also led a team of four ear surgeons and a head nurse, and operated on 27 ears of 22 patients in JDWNR hospital during a four-day camp in May.

The team also donated an operation room television monitor to the hospital. The team brought all of the equipment and materials required for the campaign.

"The advantages to this method are that there is only a minimal need for post operation care, and the operation is quick compared to others," he said.

Dr Phub Tshering, an ENT surgeon with the JDWNR hospital, said that Bhutan could not afford to conduct such operations. "It's a very expensive technique, and we're resorting to cheaper ways, which require more post operation care, but are equally effective," Dr Phub said.

The camp has reduced the number of patients waiting for operations, which otherwise would not have been performed until April next year.

According to him, discharging ear is the cause of the perforation of the eardrum in most Bhutanese. The discharge accumulates and causes infection, which perforates the eardrum.

"Any discharging ear should be seen by an ENT specialist at the earliest possible to make proper diagnosis and determine what needs to be done," Dr Phub said.

However, he said about 80 percent of the cases do not require an operation. "This, however, has to be determined by a doctor," he said.

Meanwhile, while the doctors are busy in the operation room, Nima Choden anxiously waits outside. She had an operation four months ago. "I suffered for nine months before I went under the knife at the Thimphu referral hospital, but my ear's not cured," Nima, from Nganglam in Pemagatshel, said.

After rushing from one referral hospital to another, and swallowing hundreds of anti-biotic pills, she was registered for this operation.

"I heard the surgeons are very experienced, so I'm looking forward to being cured," Nima said.

Other patients said they began to hear gradually upon completion of their operations.

The team will continue to hold similar camps for the next two years, and is scheduled to return to Bhutan in September 2014.

Structure & Writing Expression

＜付帯状況の with の働き＞

多くの情報を詰め込み、文章を引き締める「付帯状況」の with ～ in ...、with ～ 過去分詞、with ～ ing（～が＜いま＞…の状況に置かれていることから判断すると）の構文。

（例―1）"**With** Brazil in the state it's in, I know they are doing the right thing."
（「いまブラジルの置かれている状況から判断すると、彼らのやっていることは、間違いないのだ、と思う」）

（例―2）... **with** fewer single men and couples and families making the journey to the Far East.
（極東に旅行する独身者、カップル、家族の人たちの数がますます少なくなっている＜ことから判断して＞）

本文では：But **with** one of his ears blocked since college days, listening to people was always a trouble.

Comprehension

本文の内容と同じものは T、異なるものには F と答えなさい。

1. (　) Teknath's operation in India cured him.
2. (　) All of the members of the Japanese surgery team are from Sendai.
3. (　) Surgical gadgets were provided free of charge by a Japanese surgeon.
4. (　) This camp for ENT surgeries was conducted for the first time in 2013.
5. (　) ENT surgeons in Bhutan have as effective a technique as Japanese surgeons have.

Word Check 2

下線部と同じ意味となるものを記号で選びなさい。

1. "I still kept suffering from infections quite frequently, ...
   (a) began   (b) stopped   (c) continued

2. The team consists of four senior surgeons; two from Sendai ...
   (a) recruits   (b) sponsors   (c) constitutes

3. The team also donated an operation room television monitor to the hospital.
   (a) contributed   (b) brought   (c) introduced

4. "This however, has to be determined by a doctor," he said.
   (a) must   (b) can   (c) may

解説

　仙台の耳鼻科医院を中心とした医療チームがブータンの首都ティンプーで3日間の予定を組んで医療活動を開始。25人の患者が手術を受けた…この事を報じた記事であるが、まず第一に日本の医療水準の高さと、手術の素早さに驚いた様子を伝えている。

　インドの病院で治療を受けたのにもかかわらず、経過が良くなかった患者が一時間もたたないうちに手術を終え、術後の経過が良好である事、また国内の病院で治療を受けていた女性患者の話などを取り混ぜる手法で、日本の医療技術の高さを具体的に表現。更にはこのチームが1万ドルの医療器具を寄付してくれる事も喜びを込めた表現で伝えている。

　なぜ日本の医療チームがティンプーに来たかについてチームリーダーのコメントを挙げ、東日本大震災に対するブータン国民の支援活動に報いるためであった事を明らかにし、日本人の感謝の気持ちを読者に伝えようとしている。

　ブータン王国は東日本大震災義援として8,200万円を贈ってくれた。震災当時、2011年の統計によるとブータン王国のGDPは14億ドル。これは日本の人口5万人程度の市町村に相当する経済規模でしかない。ブータンにとってはこの金額を日本に贈るのはどれほどの事であったのか想像に難くない。そればかりか、2011年11月にはワンチュク国王が結婚したばかりのペマ王妃を伴い震災後初の国賓として日本を訪問された。国王は国会で演説をし、ブータン国民が日本の復興を心から祈っている事を切々と述べられたのである。

　ご夫妻は被災地にも足を運ばれ、積極的に避難所を訪問し、被災した人達に直接お声をかけられた。この若い国王ご夫妻のさわやかな笑顔と心強い言葉は日本人に勇気を与え、ブータン王国そのものが日本人に強く印象付けられ、一時、テレビのワイドショーなどを通じてブータン王国ブームが起きた事も記憶に新しい。経済援助だけではなく、この記事で紹介されている様な、日本の特性を生かした援助を通じて震災支援へのお返しを続ける事こそ、互いの心の絆を強くする事がこの記事から感じ取れる。

Unit 14

Japan's Clothing Retailer Uniqlo to Buy More from Bangladesh

The Daily Star（バングラデシュ）June 21, 2013

Close-up

ユニクロは内外に多数の店舗を持つアパレル業界の大手。近頃では海外進出も目覚ましい。親会社ファーストリテイリングの売上高は世界第四位を誇る。

Punch Line

> "But the garment makers should remember that it's all about quality for the average Japanese consumer. As long as they satisfy the quality-conscious Japanese customers, orders will flow in."

(「でも、衣料メーカーは、品物の質こそ平均的な日本人の消費者にとってすべてである、と認識すべきだ。品質にうるさい日本人の消費者を満足させれば、注文は殺到する」)

Word Check 1

(1)～(10) の語・句の意味として最も適当なものを選択肢 (a)～(j) の中から選びなさい。

(1) retail
(2) disclose
(3) garment
(4) quality
(5) announce
(6) implement
(7) primary investment
(8) domestic
(9) selling target
(10) fiscal year

(a) 衣服
(b) 小売
(c) 会計年度
(d) 品質、良質な
(e) 国内の
(f) 実施する
(g) 開示する
(h) 売り上げ目標
(i) 初期投資
(j) 告知する

Japanese retail giant Uniqlo plans to bolster its garment order volume from Bangladesh, a top official of the company said.

"I do not want to disclose the volume though, as it's a business secret," Yukihiro Nitta, group executive officer of Fast Retailing, Uniqlo's parent company, told The Daily Star in an interview.

The company has decided to divert 30 percent of its annual purchases from China to Bangladesh, Thailand, Vietnam, Indonesia and Cambodia.

Bangladesh will be a "significant" beneficiary of this decision, Nitta said.

"But the garment makers should remember that it's all about quality for the average Japanese consumer. As long as they satisfy the quality-conscious Japanese customers, orders will flow in."

Nitta praised the country's garment workers, describing them as "hard-working" and capable of producing "quality" merchandise. "We're very satisfied with their work," he said.

Nitta was recently in Dhaka to announce the opening of two Uniqlo stores in collaboration with Grameen Healthcare Trust, based on Professor Muhammad Yunus' much-praised social business model.

The stores, to be branded as Grameen Uniqlo, will take off on July 5, targeting the under-35 consumer demographic.

The seed for the partnership has been in germination for three to four years, he said.

Yunus was addressing a seminar in Tokyo, which was attended by Tadashi Yanai, chairman of Fast Retailing.

"He [Yanai] was so inspired by the social business model that Professor Yunus talked up, that he started looking right away for business ventures to implement the idea. Finally in 2011, this opportunity with Grameen Healthcare Trust came up — and Fast Retailing jumped on it."

Established in August 2011, with a primary investment of USD $4.6 million, Grameen Uniqlo would 99 percent be owned by Fast Retailing, and 1 percent by Grameen Healthcare Trust.

Products to be sold at the two stores would be designed by the company itself in Japan, but would be manufactured in Bangladesh. "But I will not disclose the names of the factories," Nitta said.

Nitta says the Grameen Uniqlo outlets, where the prices would vary from $2.5 to $15.5 per item, would not be competing with the growing domestic garment brands.

"Rather, we will deliver innovations in design and fashion to the middle-class customers of Bangladesh. We have an annual sales target, which will be made public later."

Regarding Uniqlo's refusal to sign the fire and safety accord designed by IndustriALL, he said: "We have the willingness to continue doing business here for a long time, so we will implement our own safety measures in the factories that we source from."

Fast Retailing is currently the world's fourth largest apparel company, with global sales for the fiscal year that ended on August 31, 2012 at 928 billion yen (approximately $9.5 billion). The company has 1,206 stores in 13 markets, at present.

---

accord 協定

IndustriALL ジュネーブに本部を置く労働組合の国際組織

safety measures 安全対策

Structure & Writing Expression

＜ HEADLINE（見出し）の語法：to+ 動詞の原形は未来を表す＞

Japan's Clothing Retailer Uniqlo **to Buy** More from Bangladesh

未来を表すのには "to+ 動詞の原形" の形が最も一般的である。この見出しは、"be+to+ 動詞の原形" の be 動詞が省略されたものである。もちろん未来を表す助動詞 will, shall とか be about to 動詞の原形が用いられることもある。

（例） U.S. **to Lift** Sanctions against South Africa
　　　（米国、南アフリカに対する制裁を解除の予定）

見出しは次の記事のように、lead paragraph（記事の最初のパラグラフ＜原則として 5W (who,what,when,where,why) IH (how) を含む＞）から取られる。

WASHINGTON (Reuter) – The United States **is about to lift** most of its economic sanctions against South Africa...

Comprehension

本文の内容と同じものはT、異なるものにはFと答えなさい。

1. (　) Uniqlo has never imported apparel from Bangladesh.
2. (　) Nitta said garment workers in Bangladesh are diligent and competent enough to produce quality garments.
3. (　) Grameen Healthcare Trust invested almost all of $4.6 million.
4. (　) Products are all designed and manufactured in Bangladesh.
5. (　) Uniqlo has stores in more than a dozen countries.

Word Check 2

下線部と同じ意味となるものを記号で選びなさい。

1. The company has decided to <u>divert</u> 30 percent of its annual purchases from China to Bangladesh, ...
   (a) implement (b) increase (c) switch

2. The stores, to be branded as Grameen Uniqlo, will <u>take off</u> on July 5, targeting ...
   (a) disclose (b) open (c) announce

3. Nitta says the Grameen Uniqlo <u>outlets</u>, where the prices would vary ...
   (a) exits (b) stores (c) companies

4. "We <u>have the willingness to</u> continue doing business here for a long time, so ..."
   (a) will (b) decide to (c) intend to

解 説

　世界第4位のアパレル会社ファーストリテイリングが経営するユニクロがバングラデシュの縫製（ほうせい）技術を評価して取引を大幅に増大するという記事。今後、バングラデシュの主要産業として縫製業が大きく成長する事を期待する明るい色調に満ち溢れている。バングラデシュではここ10年近く安い労働力を基礎に縫製産業が育ってきており、取引先はアメリカやヨーロッパが主で、それなりに技術を向上させていたのである。

　ところが最近風向きが変わった。中国に生産拠点を持っていた、日本の中小アパレル業が、賃金の高騰や反日気運の高揚が主な原因で撤退を始め、バングラデシュに中心を置き始めたのだ。これまで中小の日本アパレル企業の進出はかなり早い時期からあり、日本の細やかな生産技術が現地の工場に伝えられ、生産品も高度なものができ上がる素地が培（つちか）われてきていた。そこにユニクロが本格的に進出し、大幅な経済効果をバングラデシュにもたらすようになったのである。

　しかし、急速な発展にこの国のインフラが追いつけず、大量の電力消費を賄いきれずにたびたび停電が発生、生産品が納期に間に合わない事もある。更には2013年、古いビルに大量の従業員と縫製機械を詰め込んだ事が原因でビルが崩壊し、若い女性を中心とした従業員が数多く死傷するという事件も起きている。このように、かつて日本にもあった女工哀史（あいし）のような過酷な労働を強いる状況が存在しているのも事実である。ユニクロの進出とその経済的効果を喜ぶのはわかるが、その裏面にある自国の現状も採り上げて改善を主張する姿勢があればこの記事はもっと充実したものになっただろう。

Unit 15

Speaking the Same Language
— Cultural Ties between India and Japan Have a Long, though Quiet, History

The Indian Express（インド）December 10, 2013

Close-up

天皇ご夫妻のインド訪問は、両国の文化交流に多大なる貢献をしたと思われる。「インド国際センター」設立の基盤は、1960年、天皇（当時は皇太子）ご夫妻の訪問中に置かれた。センターはそれ以来インドと他国との交流を深めることになった。さらに日本からの経済的支援は高度な学術研究の増進となり、日本への留学が活性化されることが望まれている。

Punch Line

> There have been misunderstandings because of the lack of timely dialogue between the two countries, but never a period of outright hostility.

（日印両国間に適宜的な対話が不足していたため、誤解が生じたが、絶対的な敵意に至ったことはなかった）

Word Check 1

(1)～(10) の語・句の意味として最も適当なものを選択肢 (a)～(j) の中から選びなさい。

(1) bilateral　　　　　(a) 交流する
(2) interact　　　　　(b) 目的地
(3) empathy　　　　　(c) 重大な
(4) scholarship　　　 (d) 自由化する
(5) discourage　　　 (e) 共感
(6) destination　　　 (f) 新規構想
(7) liberalize　　　　 (g) 両国間の
(8) momentous　　　(h) 政策
(9) initiative　　　　 (i) 奨学金
(10) policy　　　　　 (j) 思いとどまらせる

75

The emperor and empress of Japan's recent trip to India is a landmark in the history of bilateral ties between the countries. For the couple, the visit would have been tinged with nostalgia — the last time they were in India was for their honeymoon in 1960. During that trip, they laid the foundation stone for the India International Centre in New Delhi, which has since become well known for organising programmes on art and culture, as well as seminars and conferences to promote understanding between India and various other nations, including Japan. During a more recent visit here they visited Kalakshetra in Chennai, indicating their keen interest in Indian art and culture. Apart from meeting dignitaries, they also interacted with various sections of people in India — academics, artists, scientists, schoolchildren. Japanese nationals in India also enjoyed a rare opportunity to interact with the emperor and empress.

The visit signifies the growing importance Japan has accorded to India in all spheres and the greater interactions between the people of both countries to promote mutual understanding. While our postwar relations with Japan started on a note of mutual respect and empathy, its decision to ally with the US while India preferred to remain non-aligned drew the two countries apart. However, even in this period of distance, certain ties survived. Japan was the first country to extend aid to the tune of $50 million to India, as early as in 1958. India continued to hold first place in Japan's overseas development assistance grants and loans programme, used for infrastructure development.

The notion that good relations between nations can only be built on mutual understanding and respect led to India and Japan offering scholarships for higher studies in all fields to those who wished to study in the other country.

There is no doubt that, because of Japan's phenomenal economic growth, it was able to contribute more to this endeavour. However, the Euro- and US-centric attitudes of Indians often discouraged them from opting for Japan as a higher education destination. The normalisation of Japan's relations with China in 1972 opened up the latter as a destination for Japanese investment and products. India's importance to Japan therefore declined.

There have been misunderstandings because of the lack of timely dialogue between the two countries, but never a period of outright hostility. The prompt assistance Japan gave India to tide it through the

1991 balance of payments crisis opened up a new phase in bilateral ties. Soon after, India launched its Look East policy and liberalised its economy. India's economic reforms were promoted in Japan by its media and several economic organisations. Large Japanese companies, such as Toyota, Mitsubishi and Sony, established a presence in India. In spite of opposition from China, Japan made the momentous decision to support India's becoming an integral part of the East Asia Summit.

On the cultural front, the Japan Foundation — a counterpart to the Indian Council for Cultural Relations — established an office in India in 1994 and facilitated an increased number of academic and cultural exchanges. Even as early as 1910, Japanese universities offered courses in Indian languages. But the study of the Japanese language — a means to understand the development and various other aspects of the country — only started in the late 1950s in India. It was only in 2004, as a result of initiatives to promote economic relations between the two countries, that a definite target for the promotion of Japanese language education in India was set. It was decided that Japanese could be introduced even at the secondary level in schools in India, to help students overcome the language barrier. As a part of its globalisation policy, Japan started the Global 30 programme, in which select Japanese universities will impart education in English. Scholarships have also been instituted. However, Japan is still not viewed as a destination for higher education among young Indian students, who still look towards the West, particularly to English-speaking countries.

It is hoped that the recently concluded visit will facilitate a change in attitudes and there will be more interactions between the young of both countries. This will promote mutual understanding and the realisation that we have many similarities in our traditions and values.

By Savitri Vishwanathan—*The writer is a former professor of Japanese studies, University of Delhi.*

Structure & Writing Expression

<分詞構文>

〔文頭、文中、文尾に神出鬼没して、主節（主役）を引き立てる「名脇役」の分詞構文〕

接続詞を用いた文は、とかく冗長になりがちなので、新聞では分詞構文が多用される。特に例文のように、分詞構文の意味上の主語が前の文章の内容全体であったりするので注意が必要である。

（例文）

Between 10, 000 and 25,000 people were at the site Thursday night gazing at the white billboard, **causing** traffic jams.

（1万から2万5千人の人々が木曜日夜、その場所に集まってその真白な広告掲示板を見つめていたため、交通渋滞を引き起こした）

本文では：During a more recent visit they visited Kalakshetra in Chennai, **indicating** their keen interest in Indian art and culture.

Comprehension

本文の内容と同じものはT、異なるものにはFと答えなさい。

1. (　　) The emperor of Japan has visited India once a decade.
2. (　　) There was a period when Japan and India were estranged.
3. (　　) In the 1990s, large Japanese companies expanded their business to India.
4. (　　) It was just ten years ago that Japanese universities offered Indian language courses.
5. (　　) More Indian students choose English-speaking countries as a destination for higher education.

Word Check 2

下線部と同じ意味となるものを記号で選びなさい。

1. <u>Apart from</u> meeting high dignitaries, they also interacted with various sections of people in India ...
   (a) besides　　　　　(b) far from　　　　(c) in spite of

2. The visit signifies the growing importance Japan has <u>accorded to</u> India in all spheres, and ...
   (a) given　　　　　　(b) agreed with　　　(c) promoted

3. India's importance to Japan therefore <u>declined</u>.
   (a) increased　　　　(b) decreased　　　　(c) finished

4. ..., Japan made the momentous decision to support India's becoming an <u>integral</u> part of the East Asia Summit.
   (a) essential　　　　(b) comprehensive　　(c) unnecessary

解説

　2013年、二度目にインドをご訪問された天皇ご夫妻の事を採り上げてインドと日本の親密な関係を歴史的経緯も含めて記述しているインド紙の記事。この記事全体を通じて印象的なことは日本と、日本文化の象徴としての天皇ご夫妻を尊重する記述が随所に見られる事である。更にはインド文化と日本文化の比較と共通点を通して互いに長い歴史と伝統を持つ同じアジアの国としての共感を分かち合おうとする態度に満ち溢れている事がこの記事から感じ取れる。

　記事の中では、1960年、天皇(当時は皇太子)ご夫妻が最初にインドを訪問された時はお二人のハネムーンであった事、その時ご夫妻がインド文化に大変な興味を持ち、首相をはじめとする政府高官とお会いになった後、各階層の文化人や学者、アーティストなどと親しく面談された事など紹介し、日本の天皇家が明るくオープンである事、今回のご訪問も前回と同じようにインドに対して親しみと尊敬の念を抱いている事を全面的に強調。日本そのものにインド人も共通した感情を持っている事を示そうとしている。

　第二次世界大戦後、復興した日本が最初に経済援助を行った国がインドである。言わば新生日本が最初に具体的な外交行動の対象としてインドを選んだのであり、その事が戦後に於けるインドと日本の長い親交の基礎となっている。しかしながら、この記事の中では、1972年、日中国交正常化以降日印関係が疎遠となり、現在に至って中国との関係がギクシャクしている事で日印関係が親密度を増したと解説しており、日本の経済中心の外交姿勢についての批判もしている。その事をふまえると、日本にとっては現実的な利害関係だけではなく、末長い日印の親交を深めていく事が今後の課題となるだろう。

Unit 16
Buddhist Values Can Thwart Threats to World Peace

The Daily News（スリランカ）December 20, 2013

Close-up

大衆部（大乗仏教の別称）の日本と上座部（小乗仏教の別称）のスリランカは、宗派は異なるが、仏教の基本的理念は同じである。両国の歴史的関係は仏教を基盤としており、その他の国々にもこの仏教的精神が浸透すれば、世界は平和になるだろう。日本の日蓮宗総本山（久遠寺）とスリランカのウエラワッタ国際仏教センターが世界平和に向けて主導権を握る。

Punch Line

> "Our country stood by Japan honestly. Japan was endowed with prosperity and freedom followed by the speech made by J.R. Jayewardene in San Francisco, referring to the Buddha's preaching that 'hatred cannot be doused by hatred.' Gratefulness is still there in the minds of the Japanese people."

(「我が国、スリランカは日本を心から擁護した。'怨みに報いるに、怨みをもってせず' と説く法句経をサンフランシスコ講和条約で、引用した J.R. ジャヤワルダナ（のちに首相・大統領）の演説に従い、日本は繁栄と自由を賦与された。感謝の念が今もなお日本国民の心の中にある」）＜旧日本軍はコロンボとインド洋に面したセイロン島のトリンコマリーなどを空爆したが、スリランカ（当時セイロン国）は日本から賠償を一切要求しなかった＞

Word Check 1

(1)〜(10) の語・句の意味として最も適当なものを選択肢 (a)〜(j) の中から選びなさい。

(1) thwart
(2) tribute
(3) sponsorship
(4) confront
(5) relief
(6) privilege
(7) penalize
(8) nurture
(9) comprehend
(10) bestow

(a) 後援、資金提供
(b) 罰する
(c) 妨げる、防ぐ
(d) 育てる
(e) 救援
(f) 名誉
(g) 与える
(h) 賛辞
(i) 理解する
(j) 〜に直面する

"The day that the powerful people of the world understand the values of Buddhism, threats to world peace can be thwarted," President's Parliamentary Affairs Secretary Kumarasiri Hettige said.

"The basis of the historic relationship between Japan and Sri Lanka is Buddhism and if such ties exist among all nations, the world would be a peaceful place to live," he said.

Hettige was speaking as the chief guest at a function held at Wellawatte International Buddhist Centre on December 15, to pay tribute to International Affairs Director of Minobu Temple, head office of Nichiren Sect, Ven. Akiyoshi Yoshimura Thera.

The function was held in appreciation of the support extended by Minobu Temple in favour of the religious and social services carried out by the Chief Incumbent of Wellawatte International Buddhist Centre, Ven. Maharagama Mahinda Thera. The Montessori project named Minobusan is also operated with the sponsorship of the 'Minobu' temple of Japan.

Hettige said: "The Japanese society is a fine model for countries like Sri Lanka. The relationship between the two countries is historic. The world still remembers how Hiroshima and Nagasaki, cities in Japan, were destroyed with nuclear bombs during the Second World War. Japan had to confront an unexpected catastrophe.

"Our country stood by Japan honestly. Japan was endowed with prosperity and freedom followed by the speech made by J. R. Jayewardene in San Francisco, referring to the Buddha's preaching that 'hatred cannot be doused by hatred'. Gratefulness is still there in the minds of the Japanese people.

"Whenever we are confronted with a disaster, Japan helps us. When the Tsunami devastation occurred in 2004, Japan was in the vanguard to provide relief to the affected. When the military operations were carried out to conclude the 30 year war, Japan performed the role of a sensible arbitrator, irrespective of international pressure. Yasushi Akashi still visits Sri Lanka, and shows support for the President. Japanese monks bestow blessings on the President. The secret behind this relationship is Buddhism.

"Paying tribute to Ven. Akiyoshi Yoshimura Thera is a great privilege. He has shown a great compassion towards the children of our country. Certain superpowers with colonial thoughts are making efforts to penalise our country for defeating terrorism and ushering in peace.

"They pave the way for separatism and terrorism to raise their ugly heads again. They intervene in our country's internal affairs unnecessarily. Is this moral? Our country has advanced greatly since the President was appointed as the Chairman of the Commonwealth.

"There also the President referred to the Buddha's preaching and stated not to find others' faults but find the faults within themselves, wisely.

"That is good advice for any state or person. Now Sri Lanka is becoming a beautiful country. Buddhism is being nurtured, and temples are being developed. Many have started to think of a religious life. The mental development of the people also should keep the same pace with material development. So prathipaththi pooja (practice of dhamma) should be given first place rather than amisa pooja (practice of offerings).

"In order to build world peace, there should be world leaders who comprehend the teachings of the Buddha. Sri Lanka and Japan are exemplary nations. President Mahinda Rajapaksa works diplomatically, setting an example for most world leaders."

Ven. Akiyoshi Yoshimura Thera said Sri Lankans are kindhearted.

"We love Sri Lanka a lot. We are glad that we're able to help Sri Lanka. We gladly accept the tribute bestowed on Minobu Temple. We appreciate the services rendered by monks like Ven. Maharagama Mahinda. We feel very happy about the steady development taking place in Sri Lanka. We wish that the links between the two countries will be strengthened further," he said.

Ven. Maharagama Mahinda Thera said he was able to accomplish a great service to Sri Lanka with the help of Minobu Temple while he was in Japan, studying Mahayana Buddhism.

Structure & Writing Expression

＜絵画的効果が鮮烈な文頭の副詞句＞

まずは「副詞句」を前に出して、文を引き締める。

（例 -1） **On a hill overlooking the ocean** stands a magnificent cathedral.

（例 -2） "**To understand the Japanese people and culture**, the first step is language," says he.

本文では："**As to build world peace**, there should be world leaders who comprehend the teachings of the Buddha."

Comprehension

本文の内容と同じものは T、異なるものには F と答えなさい。

1. (　　) The relationship between Japan and Sri Lanka has only just begun.
2. (　　) President J.R. Jayewardene made a speech in favor of Japan.
3. (　　) Some countries attempt to promote separatism and terrorism in Sri Lanka.
4. (　　) Many Sri Lankans are conscious of religion.
5. (　　) Politicians should learn the teachings of the Buddha.

Word Check 2

下線部と同じ意味となるものを記号で選びなさい。

1. Hettige was speaking as the chief guest at <u>a function</u> held at Wellawatte International Buddhist Centre ...
   (a) a role (b) an event (c) a place

2. When the Tsunami devastation occurred in 2004, Japan <u>was in the vanguard</u> to provide relief to the affected.
   (a) was among the first (b) was in the group (c) was the last

3. Certain super powers with colonial thoughts <u>are making efforts</u> to penalise our country for defeating terrorism and ushering in peace.
   (a) are reluctant (b) are attempting (c) are able

4. There also the President <u>referred to</u> the Buddha's preaching and stated "not to find others' faults but find the faults within themselves, wisely."
   (a) remembered (b) denied (c) cited

解説

　日本の仏教団体と共同で祭事があった事を報じながら、日本とスリランカの長い間の関係の深さに言及するという流れの記事である。この記事で特徴的な事は良好な両国関係の背後に根差しているのは同じ仏教国としての宗教的価値観である…としているところだろう。

　事実、この記事でも触れられている J.R. ジャヤワルダナ氏（後に首相・大統領）と日本との関係は仏教を抜きには語れないところがある。ジャヤワルダナ氏はキリスト教から仏教に改宗した人物で、1951年のサンフランシスコ平和条約締結時セイロン（現スリランカ）代表として会議に参加。第二次世界大戦中セイロンは英国の植民地であり、首都コロンボが日本軍の爆撃を受けており、英国から独立後対日平和条約締結国の地位にあった。

　この会議中、ジャヤワルダナ氏は「憎悪は憎悪によって止むことはなく、慈愛によって止む」とのブッダの言葉（法句経）を引用して、セイロンは日本に戦時賠償を請求しない事を宣言した。これに関係各国が同調し、日本は賠償を免れ、戦後復興に全力を注ぐことが可能となった。1996年の死亡後、遺言によって彼の右目の角膜はスリランカ人に、左目のそれは日本人に提供されている。これら一連の事実はスリランカの教科書に記載されており、スリランカ国民全てが知っている事だが、日本人では知る人は少ないだろう。

　この記事では仏教の平和主義が基調となれば、世界中で争いがなくなるとしているが、スリランカでは1983年から2009年まで実に26年の長きに亘って人口の70%を占める多数派シンハラ人（仏教徒）と20%の少数派タミル人（ヒンズー教徒）との間に内戦があった。最終的には海・空軍まで投入してシンハラ人の政府軍が勝利したが、記事の中でことさら仏教思想を強調しているのは勝利した仏教徒の高揚感の残滓と言えなくもないだろう。

Unit 17

Japan's PM Pushes India Ties amid Sino-Japanese Tensions

The Daily Times（パキスタン）January 26, 2014

Close-up

安倍首相は、あたかも「日本株式会社」のセールスマンのように世界を駆け巡っている。今回は、中国の東シナ海の勢力拡大を牽制するため、インドを訪問、日印両国の経済的及び安全面での関係を一層固めるための決意表明を行った。

Punch Line

> Abe told a business audience late Saturday that relations between India and Japan could be "win-win" and offer India "some of the best technology."

（安倍首相は、先の土曜日、ビジネス界の聴衆に向けて、日印関係は「双方に満足できる」ものであり、「何らかの最高の技術」を提供できるだろう、と語った）

Word Check 1

(1)~(10) の語・句の意味として最も適当なものを選択肢 (a)~(j) の中から選びなさい。

(1) offset
(2) simmer
(3) vital
(4) outbreak
(5) hit back
(6) delegation
(7) showcase
(8) nuclear
(9) military
(10) capital

(a) 発生、勃発
(b) 軍事用の
(c) 反論する
(d) 資本
(e) 相殺する
(f) 原子力の
(g) くすぶる
(h) 披露する
(i) 代表団
(j) 必要不可欠な、重要な

85

NEW DELHI: Japan's Prime Minister Shinzo Abe arrived in New Delhi on Saturday to push for closer commercial and strategic ties with India, as Tokyo seeks to offset Beijing's growing regional might.

Since coming to power in 2012, Abe has trotted the globe, partly in his self-appointed role as salesman for Japan Inc., but also to seek counterweights to superpower China.

Abe told a business audience late Saturday that relations between India and Japan could be "win-win" and offer India "some of the best technology".

Earlier Abe told The Times of India in an interview published Saturday he wants to "develop vigorously" economic and security cooperation with India.

Abe's speech avoided any mention of Japan's bitter territorial row with China over islands in the East China Sea that Asia's two largest economies both claim.

He urged Beijing on Friday to come to the table for "vital" summit talks, after being quoted as comparing current Japan-China relations with ties between Germany and Britain before the outbreak of World War One.

China's Foreign Minister Wang Yi on Saturday hit back at Abe's claim about tensions in East Asia, saying the analogy was misplaced.

"The forces for peace in the world, and they include China, are growing," Wang told the World Economic Forum in Davos.

However, Abe told the Times of India the "security environment of the Asia-Pacific region is becoming ever more dangerous".

Japan fears China is seeking to control key shipping lanes around its vast coastline.

Japan and India, already carrying out joint maritime exercises, "play a vital role together for the security of sea lanes," Abe told the Indian daily.

India, which has its own simmering Himalayan border row with China that erupted into a brief war in 1962, has said all "regional issues" including tensions with Beijing would be discussed.

India too has been working to boost relations with Japan and other Asian nations as it seeks to offset rival Beijing's rise.

Commerce Minister Anand Sharma hailed Japan as a "very special friend of India," and expressed hopes for a deepening of the countries' strategic partnership.

Abe, accompanied by a Japanese business delegation, was making his second official trip to India and was due to attend an annual bilateral summit.

His visit follows on the heels of the first trip to India early last month by Japan's emperor and empress, billed by New Delhi as a "landmark" goodwill symbol.

Abe will be "chief guest" at India's Republic Day parade Sunday that showcases the nation's military might and cultural richness.

India and Japan will also work toward "negotiating an agreement on the peaceful uses of nuclear energy," said Gautam Bambawale, India's foreign affairs official in charge of East Asia relations.

The talks launched in 2010 slowed after the Fukushima nuclear disaster a year later, but gained momentum after the prime ministers of the two countries called for a swift conclusion.

As part of a packed agenda, Japan hopes also to push the sale of its amphibious search and rescue ShinMaywa US-2 planes.

The planes would be unarmed, so as not to break Tokyo's self-imposed prohibition on military exports.

"It will take a bit of time I am sure because defence equipment is always something difficult to transfer," said Bambawale.

But with Abe saying he wants to review Tokyo's ban on weapons exports, such a sale might open the door to Japan for sale of military equipment to India, a huge arms importer, analysts say.

New Delhi, which is seeking $1 trillion in investment over five years to upgrade infrastructure and bolster stuttering economic growth, is also looking for Japanese capital, technology and "modern management practices," said Bambawale.

Tokyo is already India's fourth-largest investor, involved in building the Delhi-Mumbai Industrial Corridor, a $90-billion project linking India's capital with financial hub, Mumbai.

Structure & Writing Expression

＜ニュース・ソース（ニュースの出所）＞

報道記事では、そのニュースの出所を明らかにすることが必要である。しかし、いつも President A said~ のように、その出所がはっきりしているとは限らない。そこで漠然とした次のような言い方が出てくる。

A quoted B as saying ~, B was quoted by A as saying ~（A は B が〜と言ったと伝えた、A が伝えるところによると B は〜と述べた、A が B の発表として伝えるところによると〜）のように他人の言葉を引用して伝えることもよくある。

（例）

French defense sources **were quoted by United Press International as saying** that …

（UPI によると、フランスの防衛筋は次のように述べた）

本文では：

,… **after being quoted as** comparing current Japan-China relations with …

Comprehension

本文の内容と同じものは T、異なるものには F と答えなさい。

1. (　　) Both Japan and India worry about China's growing power in the Asia-Pacific region.
2. (　　) There are no territorial issues between India and China.
3. (　　) India will not use nuclear energy for a peaceful purpose.
4. (　　) Exporting weapons is not prohibited in Japan now.
5. (　　) Japan has already invested in India's big industrial projects.

Word Check 2

下線部と同じ意味となるものを記号で選びなさい。

1. Abe's speech avoided any mention of Japan's bitter territorial <u>row</u> with China over islands ...
   (a) conflict   (b) line   (c) flesh

2. Japan fears China is seeking to <u>control</u> key shipping lanes around its vast coastline.
   (a) command   (b) expand   (c) develop

3. Abe, accompanied by a Japanese business delegation, was making his second official trip to India and <u>was due</u> to attend an annual bilateral summit.
   (a) was disappointed   (b) was willing   (c) was scheduled

4. The talks <u>launched</u> in 2010 slowed after the Fukushima nuclear disaster a year later ...
   (a) interrupted   (b) started   (c) scheduled

解説

　天皇ご夫妻のご訪問に続いて 2014 年 1 月末、安倍首相がインドを訪問した。この時の動向を詳細に報道したのがこの、隣国パキスタン紙の記事である。記事の中では、安倍首相には経済団体の代表が同行しており、今後 5 年間で 1 兆ドルに及ぶ日本からの投資をインドの経済相が望んだ事を伝えている。そして、これらの経済協力の中には現在海上自衛隊が使用している非武装の新明和製高性能飛行艇売却プランもある。安倍首相の構想の中には将来的に日本自らを律している武器輸出規制の解除も想定されており、日本とインドが経済と安全保障面における強い絆を結ぶ事になると予測している。

　この記事では特に、日印の安全保障連携の強化を危惧する色調が強く、安倍首相がダボス会議で東シナ海での領有権をめぐる状況を第一次世界大戦前のドイツとイギリスの関係に例えたことに言及。それに対する中国外相の、世界が平和に努力しているのにもかかわらず、それを乱すのは日本だ…という反論等を紹介する事で、全体としてはこのような日印の協力関係に反対する流れになっている。

　実を言うと、ヒンズー教とイスラム教という宗教上の違いから 1947 年、イギリスからインドとパキスタンが分離独立を果たした。その直後、カシミール地方の領有権をめぐって両国は戦争状態となり、パキスタンには中国が付きインドにはソ連がつくという複雑な背後関係となった。以降、中印は国境線を巡って戦い、更には、印パは 1999 年まで計 4 回戦争し、現在に至っている。中国とインドは 2013 年にもヒマラヤの国境線を巡って戦闘を行った。

　そのような流れの中で、この地域の安全保障上の対立はインド vs 中国・パキスタンという構図で推移してきている。この状態の中で安倍首相のインド訪問は日本とインドが安全保障面を通じて経済的な結びつきを強くする結果を生んだ。パキスタンにとって安倍首相のインド訪問は、まさにタイトルにあるように、インドを日中の緊張関係の中に押しやる事となり、結果的にはパキスタンとインド間の緊張が高まると見えているのだ。

Unit 18
Why Are the Japanese So Fascinated with Anne Frank? (1)

Haaretz（イスラエル）January 22, 2014

Close-up

日本人はどうしてこうもアンネ・フランクに魅了されるのか？アンネを見る日本人の目とヨーロッパの人たちのそれとは根本的に違うようだ。

Punch Line

For many Europeans, Anne Frank is a potent symbol of the Holocaust and the dangers of racism. But the Japanese people tend to connect to her story for fundamentally different reasons.

（多くのヨーロッパ人にとって、アンネ・フランクはユダヤ人大虐殺と人種差別の危険性の有力な象徴である。一方、日本人は、根っから異なった理由で、彼女との関わり合いを持とうとする傾向がある）

Word Check 1

(1)〜(10) の語・句の意味として最も適当なものを選択肢 (a)〜(j) の中から選びなさい。

(1) adaptation　　(a) 中立的な
(2) hideout　　(b) 隠れ家
(3) intense　　(c) 有力な
(4) atrocity　　(d) 犠牲者
(5) neutral　　(e) 翻案、改作
(6) hesitantly　　(f) 現象
(7) potent　　(g) 残虐行為
(8) phenomenon　　(h) 強い
(9) victim　　(i) ためらいがちに
(10) ignorance　　(j) 無知

She speaks only Japanese and is not entirely sure what country she's in, but 18-year-old Haruna Matsui is happy to stand in the rain for an hour with two friends to see the home of a person she has never met, yet nonetheless considers her soul mate.

"We visited Paris and Brussels, so I just had to come here to see Anne's home," an excited Matsui told JTA last week outside Amsterdam's Anne Frank House.

Matsui has read Japanese manga comic book adaptations of Frank's diary several times and watched every anime cartoon film she could find about the teenage diarist who spent two years hiding in an Amsterdam attic before her arrest in 1944.

Frank's story is so well known that dozens of nations are represented in the entry line of the museum established at her former hideout on Prinsengracht 263. Every year, more than a million people visit the museum, making it one of the Dutch capital's most visited tourist destinations.

But interest in Anne Frank is particularly intense in Japan, where her story continues to reach new audiences through comic books, cartoons, museum exhibitions and educational initiatives.

For some Japanese, this is a source of pride. But researchers who have studied this fascination say it has a dark side, reflecting a tendency to focus on Japan's victimhood during World War II while ignoring responsibility for atrocities committed by its troops who fought as allies of Nazi Germany.

Matsui thinks Japan was neutral during World War II.

"The Germans fought the French and English and the Jews in Europe, and then America and Japan had a war later," she said hesitantly through a translator.

For many Europeans, Anne Frank is a potent symbol of the Holocaust and the dangers of racism. But the Japanese people tend to connect to her story for fundamentally different reasons, according to Alain Lewkowicz, a French Jewish journalist who wrote an elaborate iPad application, "Anne Frank in the Land of Manga," about his investigation of the Anne Frank phenomenon in Japan. In January, a version of the work was published by the Franco-German television channel, Arte.

"She symbolizes the ultimate World War II victim," said Lewkowicz.

"And that's how most Japanese consider their own country because of the atomic bombs — a victim, never a perpetrator."

Currently, approximately 30,000 Japanese tourists visit the Anne Frank House every year, 5,000 more than the annual number of Israeli visitors. That figure places Japan 13th in a list whose top 10 slots are all occupied by European and North American nations.

Japan has seen the publication of at least four popular manga comic books about Anne Frank and three animated films. The first Japanese translation of Anne Frank's diary appeared in 1952, one year before it was first published in Hebrew.

"Basically, every Japanese person has read something about Anne Frank, which is even more amazing considering the shocking ignorance on history of many young Japanese today," Lewkowicz said. "The older generation has read the book, and they buy the manga adaptation for their children."

(To be continued.)

perpetrator 犯人

slot 枠

Structure & Writing Expression

<接続詞 that の省略>

口語では **that**-clause が say, think, believe, know などの目的語である場合、接続詞 that はしばしば省略される。メディアではこの省略がかなり大胆に行われ、動詞の目的語の **that**-clause だけでなく、形式主語（目的語）it によって代表される **that**-clause や so that 構文でも that が省略される傾向がある。

（例）He said he decided to issue a statement against it when it became clear* "there would be guns and shooting at any moment."

（「いつでも銃が持ち出され銃撃戦が起こる」ようなことが明らかになった場合には、それに反対の声明を出す決意であった、と彼は語った。）

本文では：

- But researchers who have studied this fascination say it has a dark side, reflecting ...

- Matsui thinks Japan was neutral during World War II.

Comprehension

本文の内容と同じものはT、異なるものにはFと答えなさい。

1. (　) Matsui read the original diary of Anne Frank, and was moved.
2. (　) Young Japanese people believe that they are victims of WWII.
3. (　) Matsui knew Japan was allied with Germany in WWII.
4. (　) The number of Japanese tourists is not as many as that of Israeli visitors to the Anne Frank's House.
5. (　) Several animated films about Anne Frank have been produced in Japan.

Word Check 2

下線部と同じ意味となるものを記号で選びなさい。

1. But interest in Anne Frank is particularly intense in Japan, where her story continues to <u>reach</u> new audiences through comic books, ...
   (a) extend　　　(b) avoid　　　(c) acquire

2. "She <u>symbolizes</u> the ultimate World War II victim," said Lewkowicz.
   (a) retains　　　(b) regains　　　(c) represents

3. Currently, <u>approximately</u> 30,000 Japanese tourists visit the Anne Frank House every year, 5,000 more than the annual number of Israeli visitors.
   (a) around　　　(b) more than　　　(c) less than

4. Japan has seen the publication of <u>at least</u> four popular manga comic books about Anne Frank and three animated films.
   (a) not more than　　　(b) not less than　　　(c) quite a little

---

解説

　2014年3月、首都圏の図書館や書店でアンネ・フランクの本が破られるという事件が発生した。この事件でTVワイドショーを始めとして、アンネ・フランクとその日記の事が採り上げられた。あらためて言うまでもないだろうが、「アンネの日記」は第二次大戦中のユダヤ人抹殺を政策として計画的に実行していたナチスに追われて最終的にはオランダ・アムステルダムの隠れ家で逮捕された当時15歳の少女の日記である。
　この記事はフランス系ユダヤ人ジャーナリスト Alain Lewkowicz 氏が書いた「漫画の国のアンネ・フランク」の分析を基礎にして、タイトルにもあるように「なぜ日本人はアンネ・フランクに魅せられるのか」を記述している。記事にもあるように、日本語しか話せない18歳の女の子がその友人とアンネの家を訪れたエピソードなどを交えつつ、イスラエルからの訪問者は年間25000人にしか過ぎないのに、日本からは30000人も来ている事実など伝え、日本人が如何にアンネに関心を持っているかを驚きのニュアンスを込めて書いている。
　記事では日本人が関心を示す原因の一つとして、アンネの日記が日本では数回にわたって漫画にされており、アニメ映画にもなっている事を挙げ、日本人の若者に認知度が非常に高いとしている。その背景には広島・長崎の被爆者と同じような戦争の犠牲者としての共感があり、かつて日本がナチス・ドイツと同盟国であり、戦争中はナチスと同じ加害者であった事が理解できていない…としている。
　更には、ヨーロッパ人にとってはアンネはホロコーストと人種差別主義の危険を表す象徴となっているが、日本人には漫画の世界の中にある…とする Lewkowicz 氏の説を引用して日本人のアンネ好きへの解説を試みる。つまり、日本人にとってはアンネフランクは「アルプスの少女ハイジ」や「メリー・ポピンズ」で描かれている漫画の世界のようなものであり、ロマンチックな空想の世界なのだと言いたいようなのだ。

Unit 19
Why Are the Japanese So Fascinated with Anne Frank? (2)

Haaretz（イスラエル）January 22, 2014

Close-up

アンネ・フランクと日本は、お互いが戦争の犠牲者である、という点で類似する。日本は原爆の被害者であり、アンネはユダヤ人大虐殺の運命に晒された。時を同じくして、日本の軍隊は韓国、中国を踏みにじり、数えきれないほどの犠牲者「アンネ・フランク」を生むことになった。

Punch Line

> "Anne Frank is a powerful symbol for peace in Japan," Otsuka said. "That's why her story resonates with so many Japanese who have suffered the horrors of war."

（「アンネ・フランクは、日本で一種の強力な平和の象徴である。それは、彼女の話が、戦争の恐ろしさを体験したかくも多くの日本人と波長が合うからである」と大塚さんは語った）

Word Check 1

(1)～(10) の語・句の意味として最も適当なものを選択肢 (a)～(j) の中から選びなさい。

(1) statue
(2) resonate with
(3) instantly
(4) juxtapose
(5) acknowledge
(6) perpetrate
(7) insincere
(8) enhance
(9) advocate
(10) comparable

(a) 高める
(b) 共感を与える
(c) 提唱する
(d) 像
(e) 犯す
(f) 即座に
(g) 匹敵する
(h) 並列する
(i) 不誠実な
(j) 認める

One place where Japanese children encounter Anne Frank's story is the Holocaust Education Center at Fukuyama City, the only such institution in the region. Run by a Japanese reverend, Makoto Otsuka, the center has welcomed 150,000 schoolchildren since its establishment in 1995.

Located just 50 miles from where the American atomic bomb landed on Hiroshima in 1945, the center is home to a statue of Anne Frank; one of only two such statues found in Japan and the only ones in her memory in the Far East. The children also tour the center's scale model of the Anne Frank House in Holland.

In 2011, the center received one of two cuttings sent to Japan from the chestnut tree Frank described in her diary. Japan is the only Asian country besides Israel with saplings from the tree. The one in Fukuyama is already nine feet tall, according to Otsuka, who spoke to JTA in Hebrew. He studied the language to improve his ability to study the Holocaust, he said.

"Anne Frank is a powerful symbol for peace in Japan," Otsuka said. "That's why her story resonates with so many Japanese who have suffered the horrors of war."

Otsuka began planning a Holocaust education center in 1971 after meeting Anne Frank's father, Otto Frank, the only member of the family to survive the war.

"What I instantly saw in the man was how much love he had, despite everything he'd been through," Otsuka said.

Introducing Japanese people to Anne Frank's story was important to Otto Frank. His efforts in this regard may be part of the reason for the Japanese interest in his daughter, according to Ronald Leopold, director of Amsterdam's Anne Frank House.

In his book, Lewkowicz juxtaposes Japan's Anne Frank fascination with what he and many others consider Japan's failure to fully acknowledge the actions of Japanese troops in areas they occupied in China and Korea.

"The Anne Frank-Japan connection is based on a kinship of victims," Lewkowicz said. "The Japanese perceive themselves as such because of the atomic bombs dropped on Hiroshima and Nagasaki. They don't think of the countless Anne Franks their troops created in Korea and China during the same years."

In Korea, Japanese troops organized the rape of thousands of enslaved Korean women who were known as "comfort women." They also perpetrated mass killings of Chinese civilians.

Japan apologized in 1993 to Korea and again in 1995 for having "caused tremendous damage and suffering to the people of many countries, particularly to those of Asian nations." But many consider the apology insufficient and insincere, citing the absence of reference to war crimes and repeated visits by Japanese leaders to shrines honoring some of the worst perpetrators. Japanese Prime Minister Shinzo Abe's visit last month to one such shrine sparked strongly worded condemnations from the Chinese government.

Otsuka says his museum is limited to the Holocaust and that other war crimes are not part of its scope. But he notes that the institution's mission statement extended to "deepening the understandings of the period and helping to enhance awareness for world peace among young people."

Despite this, Lewkowicz says that Otsuka is quietly working to raise awareness of the divisive issue of Japan's wartime record.

"Don't expect Otsuka to advocate adding the issue of Japanese war crimes to the national curriculum," Lewkowicz said. "Japan is not ready. It may seem from the outside like an ultra-liberal society, but this is a false impression."

Still, he said, "Slowly, bit by bit, Otsuka and other like-minded people are raising questions and telling people, also through the Anne Frank story, that some of what Japan did in those years is pretty much comparable."

Structure & Writing Expression

<分離不定詞>

to のついた不定詞の場合、to と動詞の原形の間に副詞が挿入されたものを分離不定詞という。この用法は一部の文法家から非難されているが、メディアの文体ではよく見かける。挿入される副詞には様態・程度を表すものが多い。

(例)

He was scheduled to **formally** announce his election intentions Sunday night.

本文では:

... what he and many others consider Japan's failure to **fully** acknowledge the actions of Japanese troops ...

Comprehension

本文の内容と同じものはT、異なるものにはFと答えなさい。

1. (　) There are two chestnut trees grown from the one Anne Frank wrote about in her diary in Japan.
2. (　) Anne Frank's story reminds Japanese people of their cruel actions in the past.
3. (　) Many Asian people think that the apology from Japan is sufficient.
4. (　) Otsuka would like to raise awareness of Japan's wartime record.
5. (　) Japanese society is tolerant towards all ideologies.

Word Check 2

下線部と同じ意味となるものを記号で選びなさい。

1. Japan is the only Asian country <u>besides</u> Israel with saplings from the tree.
   (a) except for   (b) in addition to   (c) thanks to

2. "What I instantly saw in the man was how much love he had, despite everything he'd <u>been through</u>," Otsuka said.
   (a) conducted   (b) gained   (c) experienced

3. They don't think of the <u>countless</u> Anne Franks their troops created in Korea and China during the same years.
   (a) several   (b) numerous   (c) few

4. It may seem from the outside like an ultra-liberal society, but this is a <u>false</u> impression."
   (a) right   (b) mistaken   (c) bad

解 説

　後半部分では更に日本人の歴史認識に踏み込んで、福山にあるアンネ博物館の存在（わざわざ、被爆地に近い場所にある事を強調しているところにも注目）を採り上げ、そこの館長の考え方を紹介しつつ、戦争における日本人の歴史認識の歪さを強調する手法で記事を進める。ここでは、日本が戦争中、中国や朝鮮半島を侵略し、数多くのレイプを行い、従軍慰安婦として女性を強制連行したと断定。その動かぬ証拠として、村山談話をなどを挙げ、安倍首相が靖国神社に参拝したことを中国が批判した事を付け加えている。そして、戦争の加害者であった事は無視して日本人が戦争の被害者である事をアンネ・フランクに共感する核としているると解説するのである。

　この記事は、Lewkowicz 氏の独自な視点を引用しながら、被害者、加害者の区別なく、戦争でひどい目にあった人に心を寄せる、人間として当然な日本人の心を歪なものとの印象を与えようとしているかのようだ。日本がナチス・ドイツと同盟関係にあった事は歴史的事実であり、中国（中華民国）と戦争した事も事実だ。しかし、ユダヤ人を国策として抹殺しようとした事はない。この記事の基調からすれば、ナチスに迫害を受けて欧州各地から逃げてきた 6,000 人にものぼるユダヤ人に日本通過ビザを最後まで書き続けた杉原千畝、更には、杉原のビザを正当なものと認める日本政府の決断がなければ、日本を通過してそのユダヤ人たちが逃れることはできなかったという事実をどう説明するのだろう。杉原氏の行為がことさら強調されるのが常だが、同盟国ナチス・ドイツの国策に反して日本政府がこれをバック・アップし、ユダヤ人の脱出を助けたのは紛れもない事実である。単にナチスの同盟国であった事が日本の罪のような視点は如何なものか。この記事にもあるように、アンネ・フランクはたとえ戦争中であっても犯してはならない人道上の問題を象徴するシンボルである。この事を日本人は十分理解している。

Unit 1	Alexander Mak / Shutterstock.com
Unit 2	vincent369 / Shutterstock.com
Unit 3	suns07butterfly / Shutterstock.com
Unit 5	GccDesigns Photography / Shutterstock.com
Unit 6	Gow27 / Shutterstock.com
Unit 7	idome / Shutterstock.com
Unit 8	360b / Shutterstock.com
Unit 9	Aquir / Shutterstock.com
Unit 11	Scirocco340 / Shutterstock.com
Unit 12	Hung Chung Chih / Shutterstock.com
Unit 13	DVARG / Shutterstock.com
Unit 14	MickyWiswedel / Shutterstock.com
Unit 15	ruskpp / Shutterstock.com
Unit 16	leoks / Shutterstock.com
Unit 19	catwalker / Shutterstock.com

著作権法上、無断複写・複製は禁じられています。

Asia Watches Japan 〈Revised Edition〉　　　　[B-790]
アジアから見た日本〈改訂新版〉

| 1　刷 | 2015年 2月 23日 |
| 2　刷 | 2021年 4月 10日 |

著　者　　竹村　日出夫　　Hideo Takemura
　　　　　松本　利秋　　　Toshiaki Matsumoto
　　　　　小田井勝彦　　　Katsuhiko Odai

発行者　　南雲　一範　Kazunori Nagumo
発行所　　株式会社　南雲堂
　　　　　〒162-0801　東京都新宿区山吹町361
　　　　　NAN'UN-DO Co., Ltd.
　　　　　361 Yamabuki-cho, Shinjuku-ku, Tokyo 162-0801, Japan
　　　　　振替口座：00160-0-46863
　　　　　TEL: 03-3268-2311(代表)／FAX: 03-3269-2486
　　　　　編集者　加藤　敦

製　版　　橋本　佳子
装　丁　　Nスタジオ
検　印　　省　略
コード　　ISBN 978-4-523-17790-6　C0082

Printed in Japan

E-mail　nanundo@post.email.ne.jp
URL　https://www.nanun-do.co.jp/